Succeeding in Business
without
Losing Your Faith

Succeeding in Business
without
Losing Your Faith

Edward R. Dayton

BAKER BOOK HOUSE
Grand Rapids, Michigan 49516

Copyright 1992 by
Baker Book House Company
P.O. Box 6287
Grand Rapids, MI 49516-6287

Printed in the United States of America

Library of Congress Cataloging-in-Publication Data

Dayton, Edward R.
    Succeeding in business without losing your faith / Edward R. Dayton.
    Includes bibliographical references.
    ISBN 0-8010-3015-3 (cloth) — ISBN 0-8010-3016-1 (paper)
    1. Success in business. 2. Business—Religious aspects—Christianity. 3. Business
ethics.   4. Christian ethics.
    I. Title.
HF5386.D34 1992
174'.4—dc20   92-465

For Rob

Contents

Preface

I have worked for large and small American corporations. I have worked for a Christian nonprofit agency. I have interacted with thousands of Christian leaders and Christian organizations in all six continents. Continually I struggle with the truth that in terms of human interaction there is nothing new under the sun.

Whether we set our stories in the first century or the twenty-fifth, we discover the same battles between good and evil, between our innate desire to exalt ourselves and our appreciation of the fact that there is only One who deserves such exaltation. We want to *succeed*. We want to do and be all that we ought to be.

Each of us lives out a unique life story. Each life is continually faced with a desire that in modern terms we call a drive for success. Each story is lived in a different setting, a different world. So each one of us is shaped and patterned in ways that reflect the world in which we live. In his *New Testament in Modern English*, Phillips translates Romans 12:2, "Don't let the world squeeze you into its own mould . . . " Ah, but there's the rub! How do we know what is the world's mold, and what is the image of Christ?

This is my struggle, your struggle, the struggle of every Christian: how to tell the difference between the world's mold and the image of Christ. And once we have gained some insight, how do we win the battle to be conformed to him?

This book tries to help on both counts, first, by helping us see the forces that shape the way we think and believe, the way we feel and the way we behave, and second, by suggesting ways in which we really can succeed in business without losing our faith.

Edward R. Dayton
Newport Beach, California

Acknowledgments

Years ago there was a popular song titled, "People Who Need People." The key line was "People who need people are the luckiest people in the world." I am one of those. And through the years I have been graced by many who have seen me along the way. I am grateful.

On most people's list of acknowledgments a word processor person is often the last one to thank. My experience has been the opposite. For years my faithful friend JoAnne Dawson has amazed me with her unbelievable speed and skill at the computer. But more importantly JoAnne thinks I'm great and keeps egging me on to do more and write more. Lois Curley, my literary agent, has been a warm family friend for many years, one who is always ready to respond to new ideas and believed in this book. Finally, there is my wife Marge, the other half of my life—friend, counselor, lover—who believes in *me*.

Thank you.

Is it possible to succeed in business without losing your faith? Many people don't think so. They are convinced that applying Christian principles to the workaday world of commerce will automatically limit their career potential. They believe the things one must do to "get ahead" in the job just don't fit with biblical values and are incompatible with a Christian lifestyle.

You might agree. You wish it were not so, but that's the way you've experienced it, and you don't know what to do about it. At best, you are resigned to that state of affairs. At worst, you feel helpless. You want to please God, but you think, "I've got to be realistic. I have to earn a living."

But there is something you can do to solve this dilemma. It is possible to be an effective Christian in a business-oriented society. What that requires is an understanding of the world and the forces that are working to keep our lives from being reflections of God and his purposes. "Success" can take on new meaning if we accept God's definition of the word. We can then write a new story for the rest of our lives, one that will bring us success.

Beginnings

He picked me up at the airport in Denver. Introduced himself as Roger. He was to be my chauffeur to a speaking engagement that evening. He had heard I had been an aerospace executive before going to seminary. "It must be great to do what you are doing. I wish there was some way I could get out of this rat race and really do something for God." Frustration, wistfulness, and longing were all reflected in that remark. He was in business, a "lower calling" he implied than full-time Christian service. There was something sub-Christian about business. Evidently, the "rat race" didn't leave much room for living as a Christian should.

Was he right? Had I left the dirty old business world for the much more rewarding life of working in a "Christian" profession?

America is all about business. *"The business of America is business,"* said President Calvin Coolidge in 1925, and it still is. Business is the engine that drives our economy. Business is what makes the American way of life possible. In the now famous statement of "Engine Charlie" Wilson, president of General Motors, "What is good for General Motors is good for America."

Christianity is all about Christians. The majority of the citizens of the United States say they are Christians. About 42 percent of the adult population attend church on Sunday morning and 93 percent of the homes in America have a Bible. About 38 percent of Americans say they turn to the Bible for reassurance on a regular basis. We read of current movements of the Spirit in religious revivals both within our borders and overseas. All over the country, new, dynamic mega-churches emerge, many of them designed to communicate with the "nonreligious" person. The number of how-to-be-a-good-Christian publications multiply each year.

Yet in the everydayness of life, in the getting up in the morning and facing the world before us, there are a large number of Christians who wonder whether they really *are* Christians. They plunge into a day of work on Monday in an environment that to them seems far from Christian. It feels like each day is a swim upstream against the current. They do their best to balance the rules of the business world with the rules they were taught in Sunday school or church. But the rules of business usually win. At work they are taught that to be successful, they must be a team player, to play by the rules of *this* team, to "go with the flow," and often going with the flow feels like going in the wrong direction.

Such Christians probably don't talk about it very much. It's too hard, too futile. When they come home in the evening, they don't share with their spouses the reoccurring collisions between the way they would like to live as Christians and the way they feel they have to live to be successful. And in their heart of hearts they wonder how they can do the things they do and still tell others that Jesus is Lord of their lives.

Then there are those who don't even realize that their daily lifestyle witnesses not to their Christianity, but rather to their ability to split what they believe from what they do. They believe they are Christians, but they don't live like Christians are supposed to live. Somehow they manage to live comfortably in two worlds, and easily swim back and forth between the world of business and the world they think of as Christian. They have done it a long time. Now it is a habit and they are unaware of the switch in values they make. They have concluded that to be successful this is the way they have to live, perhaps consciously, perhaps without any real thought. It is just the way things are. Church is one place. Business is another.

Looking for an Integrated Life

Do either of those descriptions fit you? They do? You are not alone. Most Christians I talk with have a tough time discovering a rewarding and integrated life—one in which life at work and life at church are based on the *same* values. Instead, day after day their goal to be successful in business and to be a successful Christian is elusively out of reach. Things just won't come together. Their lives produce a plastic kind of Christianity, one that requires playing a number of roles with differing values. It spreads from the individual into the local church in the form of a shallow hypocrisy. There is a role to be played in church and it is different from the one to be played in the business world. The inevitable disillusionment affects not only the principal players, but also entire families and congregations. Life seems divided, unrewarding. Even a weekly Bible study or prayer group doesn't seem to help.

This is a book about being a Christian in the workplace. It is a book about thinking and acting biblically in everyday life. It is as much about goals and values in a secular setting as it is about being an effective Christian. How can we square away what we believe with what we are asked to do in the workplace? For many of us the question of how can I succeed in business without losing my faith, might better be phrased as how can I *survive* in business without losing my faith!

Not a new dilemma. Christians have always found it a struggle to grow in grace, to mature, to live increasingly more God honoring, self-fulfilling lives. Saints and sages through the ages have discoursed about it. Who can number the books and Sunday morning sermons devoted to how to live a Christian life? But too often the books don't reflect our daily experience. They sound right, because the formulas seem simple and plausible. But the directives—and even the encouragements—are seldom specific to our particular situation; they don't translate principles into actions.

Every day the world of work hits us with a new predicament. Yet, when we try to apply Sunday's lessons to business decisions, or job-related issues, they don't seem to work. What are we to believe? Is Christianity just not practical in today's society? Many of us conclude it isn't. We wish it were. So we privatize our faith, claim it for our own, but fail to share it with others or activate it in our Monday-to-Friday lives.

Or maybe we believe that Christianity does have much to say about our business. We believe that its principles should work everywhere, but we don't have the energy or the courage to try. Like many good things that we know we ought to do, we can't find it in ourselves to do them. It is just too demanding, so we see ourselves as victims, caught between a rock and a hard place. On one side stand the clear demands of the Judeo-Christian ethic. On the other side are forces that apparently conspire to keep us from being what we *want* to be. Our daily failure to live up to our own expectations eventually encrusts us with such despair and guilt that we conclude that all these oughts are just not "practical" in the world in which we live.

As I talk to Christian business people about this daily struggle and about their own sense of failure in swimming against the tide, I receive a number of responses:

> "Christian ethics just won't work in the marketplace. The Sermon on the Mount doesn't fit in the world in which I work."
>
> "I have a family to support. I have to think about them."
>
> "I have to make a living, and this is the only way I know how."
>
> "It's the lesser of the two evils."
>
> "I can't always use Christian principles if I want my business to succeed."
>
> "I have to get ahead. I can't be a success if I try to apply the things I hear on Sunday to the problems I face on Monday."
>
> "I don't know how to do it any other way."
>
> "I feel powerless."
>
> "It gets tougher every day."

Worldly Values in the Church?

Perhaps some of these comments reflect your situation. What can we do about it? Is change really possible? Can life be more of a whole? Can we have the same values at work and in church, at home and in the marketplace?

This, of course, is a two-way street. If the values at work and the values in church are the same, then what we do at work should have some correlation to what we hear in church. But interestingly, there are many Christians who don't agree with that. They are afraid that trying to live with consistent values will bring "the world" into the church. They worry that instead of the church overcoming the world, the world and its values will overcome the church.

Some years ago I led an all-day planning session for our church. We had trained a team of leaders in group planning techniques and brought together over three hundred church members to work on dreams for the future. Ten groups each produced a detailed PERT plan of their ideas. (PERT is an acronym for Program Planning and Review Technique. In a number of different variations it has been used by industry to both plan projects and analyze performance.) A few weeks later I was presenting one of those blueprints to a church board. I went through the plan with excitement, explaining how the ideas all fit together and the implications for the future. When I asked for feedback, one board member was particularly outspoken: "Look, I have to do this planning stuff all day at work. Don't drag the world into this church!" He obviously felt that there was no relationship between work values and Christian values.

Who Is in Charge Here?

It is easy to talk about what we ought to do. But sometimes that can be like telling soldiers in wartime to do this or that to try to stay alive, without telling them what they are up against. Who is the enemy? Where can we expect them? What are they thinking? Instead of focusing on specific solutions that tell us, "If you do this, that will happen," we need to first look at *why* we have a problem. If we can get a better handle on what causes this seeming dichotomy between what we believe and how we behave, we will have a much better chance of taking charge of our lives as Christians, which is another way of saying that we will allow God to take charge of our lives.

God has given us all we need to write a new ending to our life story, one in which we discover success by playing according to his rules in business, in church, at home, and at play. That is really what this book is about.

In the chapters ahead we will explore how some of these feelings and beliefs came to be. We will look at success, business, and faith. We will explore the history of the secular world that threatens to over-run our society and see where and how it conflicts with the values and power of the kingdom of God. Having understood the enemy within and without, we can develop a strategy for living that will reward our efforts to succeed and also be pleasing to God.

Defining Our Terms

Let's go back to three words mentioned earlier: *success, business, faith*. We will look more deeply at them in the next chapters, but we need first to define them if we are to lay a foundation on which to build our strategy and new life story.

The first word is "success." That's a rather slippery word. One dictionary defines it this way: "Success is the degree or measure of suc-ceeding, a favorable termination of a venture, specifically the attain-ment of wealth, favor or eminence." So success refers to money and affluence (wealth), approval by others (favor), and status or fame (eminence). Or does it? Would that be God's definition of success? As we will see, our conflict is rooted in whether we are willing to allow God to define success for us, rather than accept society's criteria.

If we redefine what we mean by success, we may end up redefining lifetime goals. That sounds risky, but it is an exciting prospect! I can't do it by myself and neither can you. Indeed, it is trying to do things ourselves as self-sufficient "rugged individuals" that keeps us from the peace and contentment of true success. We need the Lord's help for that.

Obviously, success can mean many different things. We will exam-ine those particulars in the next chapter. But let me suggest what I believe is a generic definition: *to succeed is to have a sense of self-satis-faction, a feeling of rightness about what one has done, and is doing, along with the results of doing it.*

If that definition bothers you, don't bail out yet! We have been taught so long that it isn't quite Christian to focus on the self that we fail to realize it is human nature to believe that I (my*self*) am the ultimate evaluator of my success. We obviously are very conscious of what other people think of us. As Christians we are (hopefully) far more concerned with what *God* thinks of how we live. Since this evaluation takes place within the individual, if *I* am satisfied, then as far as I am concerned, I am successful. You may say that you are trying to live up to your parents' expectations of success, or your spouse's, or your boss's, or your pastor's. If you are not making it by those standards, you are not successful. But if you feel satisfied that you are doing what is expected of you, or you don't care what others expect, as far as *you* are concerned you are successful. Mind blower? Yes, to some degree. But think how wonderful it would be if all you cared about was what God thought, and you were satisfied that he was satisfied! That is mind blowing!

This is an important insight. If it is true, then the question that faces us all is not "how to succeed," but "how to be satisfied."

I started my professional life as an aeronautical engineer, and I moved rapidly through the professional ranks of engineering within a large aerospace corporation. I then moved to a smaller company in Grand Rapids, Michigan, as head of systems engineering. After five years there, our family went through one of those life-shaking, life-changing experiences. Within a matter of weeks I sensed God's call to leave the aerospace world and attend theological seminary in Southern California. My wife, my family, and I all assumed that this call I had would eventually lead me to pastor a local church. I was forty years old. I thought I had all the qualifications for being a good pastor. After all, I had considerable experience on the other side of the pulpit!

Today we would have called my seemingly radical career change a mid-life crisis. But, as my wife and I look back on the three years I attended seminary while supporting our family as a management consultant, they seem to be three of the most peaceful years of our lives. Perhaps it was partly due to the fact that I was no longer traveling as I had been in my previous occupation. Perhaps it was just the change of pace. But as I made the transition, I discovered a number of things: First, I probably had been wanting to leave the fuzzy gray world of business for the black and white world of theology. But second, I discovered that the "world of theology" is a pretty mushy gray. Third, the Lord showed me that all those years in "business" were not wasted. God could fit all my experiences together and use them to make something better. Today was the first day of my life. My past could be used to make my future successful. Finally, and most importantly, I discovered that life is a whole. It is not divided up into compartments. To talk realistically about success we need to examine every aspect of our total and ongoing life story.

When I looked back on the years that had preceded our moving to Southern California, I felt a degree of satisfaction. As far as I could tell, I had succeeded. The evidence was not just the patents I had been awarded or the technical reputation I had earned. The evidence was also a family that loved one another and loved Jesus. That was where I was supposed to be at the time and doing what I was supposed to do. I didn't need to go to seminary to learn that, and neither do you.

"Success," then, is wrapped up in all the experiences of life and how we judge them. To be satisfied with life is to be successful. To be satisfied that God is pleased with us is to be successful Christians.

The second word we must define is "business." Here Merriam-Webster tells us that the word comes from "busyness" and then goes on to define it as "usually a commercial or mercantile activity engaged in as a means of livelihood; the buying and selling of commodities or services."

But the word has broader implications. When I have asked business people what business means to them, some of the replies they have given include:

"To me its bottom line—profit."
"Beating the competition."
"It's a game to win."

When asked about some of the values they thought inherent in "business," the responses were revealing:

"If it's legal, it's okay."
"Bigger is better. We want more market share."

"People have to pull their weight, or they have to go."

"I think good business is a day's pay for a day's work."

"In business the marketplace sets the rules, and we go along with them."

In many ways those responses are hardly surprising. But contrast this business ideology with Sunday's words of love, kindness, justice, loving your neighbor as yourself, not thinking more highly of oneself than one ought to, praying about decisions, don't lie, don't cheat (steal), go the extra mile. Something wrong there.

And what about our third word: "faith"?

It's what we believe, isn't it? It is that which leads us to a place where we recognize the need for a Savior. It is that confidence that there is a God who is for us.

But faith is much more than that. The biblical idea of faith is wrapped in the results, the outcome of our belief. Faith responds to the One in whom we have faith. Faith is trust, the assumption that all things work together for good to those who love God because God says so.

We can see the two sides of faith as we compare the writings of James, the Lord's brother, and the apostle Paul. Both of them use the same example to make their point. In Romans 4, Paul wants to show us that we are made righteous by faith. He uses the example of the patriarch Abraham:

> What then shall we say that Abraham, our forefather, discovered in this matter? If, in fact, Abraham was justified by works, he had something to boast about—but not before God. What does the Scripture say? "Abraham believed God, and it was credited to him as righteousness" (Rom. 4:1–3).

James uses the same example to make a different point:

> You foolish man, do you want evidence that faith without deeds is useless? Was not our ancestor Abraham considered righteous for what he did when he offered his son Isaac on the altar? You see that his faith

and his actions were working together, and his faith was made complete by what he did. And the scripture was fulfilled that says, "Abraham believed God, and it was credited to him as righteousness," and he was called God's friend. You see that a person is justified by what he does and not by faith alone (James 2:20–24).

Both are looking at faith. Paul is saying that it is belief that establishes who we are in God's sight. The other is saying that belief is demonstrated by what we do, that faith is accompanied by right actions.

So these three—success, business, and faith—how do they fit together?

Living a successful Christian life is both a journey and a daily struggle. The question is whether we will choose "the road less traveled" or settle for a second-rate experience. We all come to forks in the road where we are tempted to take a shortcut that leads to culturally defined success.

Let's take this journey together to try to discover how for the Christian success, business, and faith do fit together.

Reflections

Each chapter ends with some questions for you to reflect on. These questions are also repeated in workbook format as the Appendix. You can answer them as you read each chapter or you can pass them by and come back to them later. You will discover "how to succeed" much sooner if you work on them as you move through the book. It will be particularly helpful to bring together a small group of Christian business friends to read this book together and share reflections.

Part 1

Elements of the Story

To be successful, we have to believe in our success. We measure success from within, from our personal point of view. Others may tell us that we are successful, but unless we are satisfied that we are, their opinions matter very little.

Most of the measurements of success that we apply to ourselves are given to us by our parents and our society. From infancy onward we look to others to decide if we are OK. When we become Christians, we face conflict if we discover that our definition doesn't agree with God's.

If we can appreciate how we came to our understanding of success, we are in a position to redefine it in a way that will please God. When that happens, we discover that we can now see ourselves as successful, not only in business, but in all of life.

1

What Is Success?

Most of us think that success can be measured by outward signs, the way the world views us. We are successful if we have accomplished our goals. We are successful if our position in society is where it ought to be. We are successful if we have provided well for our families. Some think of success in terms of having enough money. Others relate success to power or authority or status. All of these definitions are subjective, for the standards by which we measure success are ones that we either define for ourselves or allow others to define for us. Either way, they are our definitions when we accept them, sometimes unknowingly. Strangely, although other people may think we are successful and may even tell us so, unless *we* believe we are successful, we are dissatisfied.

Everyone desires self-esteem. Notice that it is *self*-esteem. We all would like to think that we are worthy of esteem. We talk about our need for a sense of self-worth. Abraham Maslow, the noted secular psychologist, in *Motivation and Personality* (1970), defined every person's ultimate goal as self-actualization. In Maslow's thinking, when we become self-actualized we have complete freedom to be and also to serve because then we no longer have to worry about who we are. Maslow was correct in saying that we have peace, we experience freedom, only when we are at peace with our self. And it is the self—*my* personal definition of success—that I have to live up to. The difference between Maslow's perspective and the biblical view is Maslow asks us to leave God out of the equation and find the source of peace within ourselves. The Bible tells us that peace and freedom are found only in Jesus Christ.

In other words, each of us would like to feel *significant*. We want to believe that the world is different because we are here. We are not happy to be another face in the crowd, another statistic on someone's graph, another driver on the freeway of life. We want to be *known* and appreciated. Again, this sense of significance is determined by how we see ourselves.

Who Defines Success?

Our definitions are not independent of the world around us, but most of us are seldom aware of how our ideas of success are shaped by our past, our present, and our vision of the future. If we can gain a better understanding of how our present ideas of success were shaped, we can set about readjusting them.

As red-blooded, independent Americans, we would all like to believe that *we* define success for ourselves. Would that were true! As much as we would like to believe that we are self-directed, most of our actions, and our evaluation of them, are dictated by others. We need others' acceptance. We want to be approved by them, affirmed by them, approved by them. We want other people to think we are OK.

Families Define Success

John Bradshaw was the host of a nationally televised Public Broadcasting System series, "Bradshaw on the Family." In his book of the same title (1988, 32), he skillfully and effectively points out how much of what we think about ourselves is shaped by the family within which we grew up. "In healthy family systems there are healthy roles. The parental role is mainly to model. Parents model: how to be a man or woman, how to be a husband or wife, how to be a father or mother, how to be in an intimate relationship, how to be functional human beings, how to have good boundaries." In other words, our parents are the first influence that defines for us what it means to be "successful" in the major roles of our lives. Blessed are those who have parents whose view of success is biblically based and whose values are integrated into a model of a complete life! Sadly, Bradshaw tells us that 96 percent of all families are to some degree emotionally impaired and hand down from one generation to the next unhealthy rules and values.

There is a great deal of talk today about "dysfunctional families," families that by their very nature and structure force children into patterns of abnormal reactions or behavior to cope with the family system. Adult children of alcoholic families are grouping together to try to understand what has happened to them. Children who have been abused often completely repress memories of what has happened to them. As adults, many of us are beginning to discover how much our childhood experiences have influenced our subsequent lives. What we are all learning is the truth of the biblical words that the sins of the fathers are visited on the children to the third and fourth generation (Deut. 5:9).

There may be many reasons, often sinful reasons, why we do the things that we do. We may blame our problems on our parents, our bad luck, our boss, or our dog. But it is our life and we have to be accountable for it. Sin—missing the mark, falling short—is our responsibility. No matter how we have been shaped by our past, at this point in life we have to accept responsibility for our future.

My eldest daughter reminded me that when she was eighteen we had a long and serious talk. I said something like, "Jill you are eighteen now. I am sure that your mother and I have made a lot of mistakes in raising you to adulthood. I am certain there are many things we could have done better. Regardless of that, you now have to take responsibility for yourself, not only for your present and future but

also for your past, and live your life as God would have you live it."
There *were* a lot of things we could have done better. Bradshaw would
say that most parents don't realize what they are doing. Many of us
are just passing on to our children a lot of the bad stuff we received
from our parents. Now each of us has to accept where we are and
move on. We have to say with the apostle Paul, "Forgetting what is
behind and straining toward what is ahead, I press on toward the goal
to win the prize for which God has called me heavenward in Christ
Jesus" (Phil. 3:13–14).

Psychologists have learned a lot about the human psyche since the
time of Sigmund Freud. Christians may decry the view of people and
the deliberate exclusion of God in Freud's theory of why we are what
we are. That debate had been going on all through this century. But
Freud's discoveries of how human beings very early in life are shaped
by their parents is now well established in our society, as well as in
Christian thought.

The popularity during the 1970s of Thomas Harris's book *I'm O.K.
You're O.K.* was a precursor of our ready acceptance of the role of the
unconscious in patterning our behavior. Harris replaced Freud's division of the personality into the id, the ego, and the super-ego, with
"child," "adult," and "parent." He used the useful analogy of the tape
recorder to help us understand that our parents recorded on "tapes" in
our unconscious a lot of information about who they thought we are
and how we should view the world. These tapes regularly play back to
us unconscious messages. Since many of these messages are wrong
or destructive, they need to be erased. Christian writers such as Ruth
Carter Stapleton and Francis McNutt have tried to help us replay these
memories and heal them. The apostle Paul knew whereof he spoke
when he called us to be renewed by the transforming of our *minds*
(Rom. 12:1–2). Many of us have a problem in bringing to a conscious
level the bad memories that lie in the unconscious. It is quite common for us to suppress childhood experiences, such as abuse from
our parents, and not realize those experiences are still affecting our
thinking and behavior. A woman who had an abusive father may be
afraid of close relationships with men. A man who as a child watched

his father routinely verbally or physically batter his mother may model the same behavior.

Our parents may have also defined success for us in somewhat less destructive ways, perhaps by firmly indicating which occupation we should pursue. How many doctors followed their parents' ambitions for them, when they would rather have been musicians? That's what happened to June, whose mother was a gynecologist and the only child in her family to earn a professional degree. When she had a daughter after having two sons, she dreamed that one day she could be just as proud of June as her parents were of her. From early childhood, June heard about her mother's achievements. June loved her mother and wanted to please her. She loved music too, but her mother saw June's skill at the piano as an adjunct to a more important profession. So June became a doctor.

How many children were kept from attending the school that most interested them because the mother or father wanted them to attend his or her alma mater? Parental dreams and pride again. Children see parents as powerful people. Efforts to please our parents, trying to live up to their standards, stay with us a long time, if not forever. That set of parental tapes plays silently (sometimes not so silently) in the data bank of our unconsciousness. "Wouldn't Dad be proud of me if he could see me now?" "I wish Mom were here. She so wanted me to . . . " Our "parent," our super-ego, keeps defining success for us, and telling us what we ought to do.

Schools Define Success

Alongside our family are other socializing institutions that define success for us. Schools have a big input. The rules of success at school are defined as a series of milestones that must be successfully achieved. Most schools ingrain in students the idea that teachers know what the rules should be. It is not our role to question what it means to be a successful student. The administrators and the teachers set up the hoops, and students are supposed to jump through them. We easily accept this system as a given of life. As educators constantly search for new ways to help us learn, they may move from disciplined style with rote memorization to a free-flowing discover-it-yourself approach. But by nature they have to define success for us because they believe their task is to make us successful. How do they (and we) know we succeeded? Remember the black robe and mortarboard? (Yours may have been a different color.) We graduated!

Society assumes that no one is really an adult until he or she has *left* school and gotten a full-time job (another milestone on the "road to success"). This was graphically brought home to me during my seminary experience. At forty, I was the oldest student that Fuller Theological Seminary had yet encountered. Most of my classmates had come directly to seminary from college. Most were headed for responsibilities as a pastor or assistant pastor in a church. In the final months of this three-year experience it suddenly dawned on me that my classmates were acting very much like college seniors. They were content to have their daily lives ordered by the routine and expectations of the seminary and to fit the rest of their lives around that. They shared the school's view that one did not really become an adult, and therefore become capable of making one's own decisions, until one had left school and gotten a full-time job.

You have to have "made it on your own" before you are deemed an adult in America. Success in school and success in a job are quite different. That may explain why so many brilliant students do poorly when they are asked to manage their own lives in a profession or business. They can measure up to the school's definitions of success but not to the outside world's.

The school's opinion of us as individuals also determines our success as a student. This has been demonstrated experimentally numbers of times when children chosen at random have been described to their new teacher as "very bright and promising." The teacher begins to treat the ones selected as though they *are* bright and promising, and they do turn out that way! You can see the same principle at work in business.

Both my wife and my youngest daughter are somewhat dyslexic. Because their brains turn things backward, they look at 123 and see 321. Both had the same experience in school. My daughter's grade-school teacher told her she would never graduate from high school. He told her she was dumb, so she felt dumb. She was convinced she was dumb. Praise God for others who convinced her otherwise. She graduated *cum laude* from college. (My wife went on to graduate from seminary when she was fifty-two and is now a practicing psychotherapist!)

Society Defines Success

Schools, of course, are part of the larger society that also has its many measures of success. We see these expectations first in society's various "classes." (How like school!) In spite of the generally egalitarian nature of American society, we do have lower, middle, and upper classes, that are based on wealth. In American thinking, lower/middle/upper are all measures of success. This is all very much a part of our American ethos and history, the effect of which we will examine in chapter 5. In some cultures, such as an earlier British society, one had an assigned *place.* To aspire to move from one's place was considered by society to be quite wrong. Not so in America. Here the general belief is that everyone should quite naturally strive to "be better," meaning to have more things, more wealth, more financial freedom, and to be someone in the society. Our American Declaration of Independence asserts that we all have a right to life, liberty, and the pursuit of happiness. Constantly we are told we need to "do better." We need a "better" house, a "better" job, a "better" title. We need "perks" to let us know we are important. The car we drive, the clothes we wear, and the briefcase we carry are all indicators of "better," which equals success.

Advertising Defines Success

For some time now billboards along major highways have been outlawed in several states. How can we get away from the continual bombardment of the media that skillfully lets us know that we are missing something in life if we don't have a certain product without which we are less than whole?

One of my simple pleasures is to tape the two TV programs we like to watch each week so that I can fast-forward past the commercials. I realize that I am missing the results of a lot of good work that runs about \$25,000 per *second* of air time to produce, but I'm happy nonetheless.

A beer commercial of some years ago summed up all the aspirations that advertising attempts to place in us: "Grab all the gusto you can get!" Hey, you deserve it! I'm not sure how you grab gusto, but obviously to be successful you had better not miss the chance to get as much of it as you can.

Advertising tells me that I can't be successful unless I look good, smell good, experience lots of wonderful things like a cruise to Alaska or the Caribbean, and above all *feel* good. It can be argued that advertising follows, rather than leads, public opinion. Advertising agencies certainly do their best to learn where our collective heads are at the moment. It can also be argued that advertising performs a valuable public function because it makes us aware of the availability of products that might be helpful to us. But advertising magnifies all the wrong images of success. It robs us of our humanity by telling us we are *not* OK and that's *not* OK.

Business Defines Success

Business is very much a part of American society. It both reflects and reinforces society's idea of competitiveness and defines success as "doing better." Growth is considered to be the desired norm. Whereas in a much earlier time we might have been content to carry out our profession to serve others and to make an adequate livelihood, we now look to others who are in the same business to discover whether or not we are performing as well as we "should." If we lose a share of the market, we worry or are discouraged. If someone else gets a promotion we expected, we are devastated. We worry even if someone else who has nothing to do with us gets a larger reward than we did.

We talk about these things with our spouses. We get caught up in this mindset as couples. Our children get drawn into the performance. Mom is in competition for next level supervisor with another woman and two men. She gets it! The family rejoices. We have *won*!

Many businesses have a "career track." They are on the lookout for promising young people whom they want to encourage. The human resources department has a special note in the file to see that this person is moved into jobs that will give broader experience and preparation for bigger things. So we speak of Liz or Martin as being "on a fast track." They are going somewhere. Liz and Martin are held up to us as role models for us. They are people on their way to SUCCESS!

Job descriptions, which are common in most businesses of any size, tell us our responsibilities and the company's expectations of us. Job descriptions are used to evaluate the value of a position. A series of grade levels is constructed. Managers are taught to motivate their employees to produce more and then reward them with "higher" positions which require even more output. Successful people are those who are moving up the corporate ladder.

But what about the person who isn't ever going to move into a more complex job (or doesn't want to)? One of my favorite employees was a woman who did her job extremely well. Florence was responsible for a database of information about strategic people. It was important to stay in touch with them. Florence faithfully kept it all current. But she wasn't going to "advance." Probably when she retired she was doing the work of two people. Was Florence successful? In whose eyes?

The Calendar Effect

Always there are other forces at work for good, for bad. Where we are right now, our immediate situation, shapes our understanding of success. We have a series of commitments that we have made, commitments to our family (single, married, children, parents), to friends, to our church. We have commitments to the bank for the mortgage on the house and commitments that we have made to our company or our social club. These commitments are promises to do something in the future. At the time we made them we expected to keep them, and so did the people to whom we committed. Our view of success is very much colored by whether or not we make our commitments and keep our promises. What could be worse than hearing, "Hey, admit it. You blew it! You said you would get it done, and you didn't."

Because knowing how well we are handling the current situation colors our thinking about success, we ask ourselves: Am I a good father? How do I know? Am I all I should be at church? Is my present situation one which my peers think is good?

Some years ago a young man came to see me. He was very upset about the way a well-known Christian brother was behaving in a certain situation. My visitor was indignant. He was outraged. In his view the leader he was concerned about was not living up to Christian standards, and he needed to be confronted with his weakness. In this young man's mind I was just the person to do it! I knew the brother. I knew him well. I also knew that there was another side to the story. But as we talked, I recognized that nothing I could say would convince my young friend. He had a set of rigid standards and he would not *compromise*! Later, as I reflected on that conversation, I was made keenly aware of the mystery of growing maturity. The strong, rather narrow opinions of the young are a needed part of growth. If you don't have strong convictions when you are young, what will you have after you have been pushed and shoved by the exigencies of life?

There are different passages and seasons of a person's life as Gail Sheey (*Passages* 1970) and Daniel Levinson (*The Seasons of a Man's Life* 1978) have reminded us. It is as though we are backing into the future, unrolling a long carpet of our past history. We see "successes" and "failures" unfold. They become part of a road map of where we have been. Future decisions are biased by previous experiences. When we are young, the road back is short and the milestones of experience are few. But as we age, the experiences increase. Some events seem to contradict others. Things that once seemed so certain because they worked out that way a number of times, are no longer givens. Much of the certainty goes out of life. We see it in the way we are willing to change our opinions. When we are twenty we *refuse* to compromise on anything. When we are thirty we are *forced* to compromise. When we are forty we *learn* to compromise. When we are fifty we discover that compromise is what life is all about.

Role Playing

The result of all of this is that the picture of what we want to be and ought to be is painted for us by our circumstances, our history, our society, and those closest to us. We respond to these portraits by molding ourselves and deciding what success means to us. Our good or bad self-images are shaped by what we hope other people will think of us. Each one of us has a public, an audience. The opinions of our parents, our siblings, our spouses, our children, our colleagues, and our fellow Christians all matter to us. We act out our lives in ways that we hope will gain their applause and their approval.

You choose a suit to wear today. You think about the meetings you will be in, the people you will see. You think about how they perceive you, how you would like them to perceive you. Your boss always seems to wear white shirts. He must like them. You're meeting with him today. Better wear a white shirt. You know that God doesn't care what you wear, but you're not thinking about what God might think. You're thinking about what your boss might think. Role playing.

You are in an important meeting. You are going to participate in decisions that will have a major impact on the future of your company. You have certain views of what the decisions should be, but it becomes quickly apparent that Liz and Martin have it figured out another way. Do you want to be on the other end of a decision? Maybe you'd better keep your opinions to yourself. The concern for others' opinion of you outweighs your concern for whether or not the decision is good, the best one for all affected by it. Role playing.

Some years ago, John Marquand wrote a book titled *Point of No Return*. The story was told from the viewpoint of one of two men competing for the vice-presidency of a bank. Each did everything he could to curry the favor of the president. The protagonist of the story finally won the promotion, but the success was bittersweet. The new vice-president suddenly saw that he could no longer live in the same comfortable, but too-small house, drive an older Buick, nor spend weekends as he cared to. Some of his current friends would have to go.

Now he had to live up to the expectations of his new role. Now he was a vice-president!

We so often know what we ought to be, what we want to be, and yet we desperately need to be what we sense others want us to be. What a quandary. When we are most aware of this, we cry out with Paul, "I do not understand what I do. For what I want to do I do not do, but what I hate I do" (Rom. 7:15). Thank God for Paul's way out: "What a wretched man I am! Who will rescue me from this body of death? Thanks be to God—through Jesus Christ our Lord!" (vv. 24–25).

The question before us is whether the most important audience is the people we are with or the One we claim to serve and worship.

Redefining Success?

At this point one could become very discouraged. Perhaps the fatalism of behavioral psychologist B. F. Skinner (1971) is all there is to life. Skinner believed that our lives are determined for us. The best thing to do is to accept that fact and live bravely. If Skinner was right, and the mess I am in is none of my own making, what hope is there for change? Might as well relax and enjoy what I can. If I am shaped by all these outside forces, what hope is there for me? Besides, why call it sin when I am the result of a lot of things other people have done? Why blame me?

I have always liked the way the apostle Paul is not afraid to bring up tough questions, the kind I always want to ask but am afraid at times to face: After having said in the ninth chapter of his Letter to the Romans that God has made us the way we are, Paul raises the question, "One of you will say to me: 'Then why does God still blame us? For who resists his will?' But who are you, O man, to talk back to God? Shall what is formed say to him who formed it, 'Why did you make me like this?'" (Rom. 9:19–20).

In the midst of this seeming determinism, God has broken into our personal histories and offered us a new life, not just a reworking of part of our life, but the possibility of living here on earth a life that is controlled by his Spirit and then eternal life with him.

Christians are assured that the One "who made all things new" desires to renew us continually. Too often we think about "conversion" as being a one-time experience. But life is an ongoing series of turnings about, of seeing things in a new way. Intellectually, most of us believe that. The task that lies before us is to understand not only God's good desires for us, but also to truly believe that the life called Christian and the life we live in business can be mutually pleasing to God.

How then should we define success? The first question of the Westminster Shorter Catechism asks, "What is the chief end of man?" The answer given is: "The chief end of man is to give glory to God and enjoy him forever." That defines our primary purpose in life and shows us where we find success. God's Word defines success as giving glory to him. If we are fulfilling that for which we are created, then we are living lives that glorify God. For the Christian that *is* success. But how can we feel successful? How can we have some assurance that what we are experiencing is success? The answer lies in the second part of the affirmation: to *enjoy* him forever. We give glory to God, and he in turn gives us the ability to enjoy him—today, tomorrow, and forever. The Christian life is intended to be a life of joy. We feel successful when we are experiencing joy. If we are loved by the Supreme Ruler in the universe, what more do we need to feel approved? If the Creator has pronounced us good, what else needs to be said? More does need to be said, because what I feel, what my heart experiences, determines my behavior.

So far, so good. But how do we go about finding and living the kind of life that glorifies God? Somehow there needs to be a connecting line, a string, a path between where we are at the moment on our journey and that ultimate goal that God might be glorified. Soon we discover it is in walking that path we find that joy of knowing God. It is in the finding of that joy that we find success, whether it be in business or in the everyday things of life.

How then shall we live? First, we need to appreciate the formidable forces that have been arrayed against us. Second, we need to gain a deeper understanding of the One who is *for* us! Third, we need to see him as the ruler of a kingdom, one which has arrived and is yet to come, a kingdom that has eternal rules and values. Fourth, in light of that we need to set about writing a new story of our own future, envisioning the life God would deem successful. Finally, we have to start living out that story, learning as we go, rewriting as necessary, but always knowing that God is for us and with us.

Reflections

We don't change easily. We have a whole set of conditions that have been built into our lives. You may have recognized yourself in much that has been said so far, but knowing and acting are not the same. Knowing something can help us change our attitudes, but we have a marvelous ability to believe we cannot change, even though we know we should. If you are serious about wanting to be successful, here is an assignment for you to complete. It won't take a lot of time, but if you do it now, what follows will be a lot easier:

1. Write the following descriptions on four different pieces of paper: First, what do you think other people think of you? Who do they say you are? Second, who do *you* think you are? Third, what and who would you like to be? Fourth, who do you think God would like you to be?

2. Read over your responses to these four questions. What do they tell you about your current perception of what it means to be successful?

3. If possible, do this assignment with a trusted friend (or better yet a group of friends). Share your answers. You will be pleasantly surprised how much you discover about each other.

Businesses differ from government and nonprofit organizations in that—whether they are providing goods or services—they view the world from the "bottom line"—profit.

Businesses vary greatly from industry to industry, in size, in shape, in their history. Where you are in your business or professional life from the vantage points of age, position, responsibility, the kind of industry you are in—all impact on how your Christianity works itself out on the job.

Why do people work in the first place? People work to make money. More importantly, they work for power, prestige, and authority—all of which the business world can give them. But God offers us a different kind of motivation. If we can base our life story on his authority and power, we will indeed be a success.

2

What Is Business?

usiness has a powerful attraction because it offers us a personal identity, possessions, prestige, and power. It gives us something seemingly worth committing our life to. What is business? Is business different from other kinds of work? Do teachers, politicians, government workers, members of nonprofit organizations face the same problems as those of us who make our livelihood in business? Is there something about the *nature* of business which makes it inherently more difficult for its participants to live a Christian life? Evidently most North Americans think so. Figure 1 shows the results of a Harris Poll, reported in *Business Week*, May 29, 1989. Not a very good opinion of business ethics!

Defining Business

What is this "business" that we are talking about? Before discussing the impact of business on us as Christians, we must define it. Business has to do with the for-profit delivery of goods or services.[1] It is the use of labor (including the owner's) or resources that are owned by the owner or the company to produce a surplus. The goal is to add

Figure 1

Americans Believe Concerning Business

Business Would . . .

Project   **Yes**

Project	Yes
Harm the environment	47%
Endanger public health	38%
Sell unsafe products	37%
Knowingly sell an unsafe product	44%
Charge inflated prices to make a profit	62%
Risk employee health and safety	42%
Do all of the above	25%
Do none of the above	8%

value to whatever it does and thus produce a return on the owner's investment. In recent years the business phrase "the bottom line" has become very much part of our vocabulary. It has come to mean, "What is the end result of all of this? What's the advantage to me or to that about which I'm concerned?" For business the bottom line is money, profit, surplus. What is the purpose of business? Most of us would reply, "To make a profit."

In a capitalist society the primary role of business is seen as making a profit, rather than meeting a need. Whereas in earlier times or other cultures each person's work was viewed as contributing to the whole, today's capitalism sees the accumulation of wealth as an end in itself. This view of making a personal or corporate profit rather than meeting a need for others is soon reflected in the attitudes of all who are involved in the business. The me-ism of the 1980s was the logical result of such a viewpoint. This leads us to the question, "What is *American* business?"

In the American system of free enterprise, "free" implies that business executives can do whatever they please within the current rules established by government, society, and/or the general industry. Legislation and custom keep changing the rules. Indeed, there are many who would claim that American enterprise is no longer free. The number of rules and regulations that operate at national, state, and local levels are so complex that if all of them were strictly adhered to, many people believe that it would be impossible to carry on a profitable business. But because most businesses operate out of public view, it is very easy to ignore or bend the rules.

The vast majority of American businesses are small, with less than a hundred employees. As they grow, they have to make up their own rules of conducting their business. Many of these rules have been shaped by the entrepreneur who began the business. Much like our parents, the founder/owner writes the "tapes" that are going to be followed in the coming years. Each business is different, and each of us has a different role in business. To know one business is not to know them all. My experience in business may be quite different from yours.

Bringing Christian Values to the Workplace

Can you succeed in business without compromising your faith? Yes, but for each of us the specific "how" will be different. Specifics will depend pragmatically on a number of things: the degree of responsibility one has for making decisions, the size of the business, the corporate culture, the way the business is organized, the industry of which it is a part and finally, how long a person has been with a company. All of these factors influence a Christian at work. Let's look at each of them.

Responsibility for Decisions

Where and when you entered a particular business and where you are right now in your leadership within that business determines your range of decision making. Obviously, the fewer daily decisions that you have to make, the fewer opportunities you have to test the business's practices against your belief system, your faith. If you are a computer programmer, for example, you may have little awareness of the kinds of ethical judgment calls that the business is regularly making. At the other extreme is the CEO who is ultimately responsible for all the decisions made within the business, and thus responsible for all of the business's values. Computer programmers may not see themselves as being able to impact their own or the public's view of their company. The CEO knows that what he or she decides can make a major difference in the company's reputation.[2]

Interestingly, in large corporations that have gained notoriety because of some illegal practice, it has almost always been the officers *below* the CEO level who have made decisions to increase profits at the expense of legality. Whose interest did they have in mind? Probably their own desire to get ahead and look good rather than making the company look good. There is something about wanting to perform well, to look good, and to be on top, that pushes people past acceptable limits. The CEO, on the other hand, can at least take satisfaction in having reached "the top," no matter how hollow the "victory" may feel.

This is not to say that you should ignore the ethical implications of what the company is about and the policies (or lack thereof) that govern its conduct. It does say that you may not be privy to the consequences of decisions being made elsewhere. Whether you should make it your business to try to learn everything that is going on is another matter. If you respect the people you report to and believe they can be trusted to make ethical decisions, then leave the questions to them. More about that later.

Corporate Culture

It is always surprising to see how companies develop different cultures, standards of conduct, ways of relating to one another, and ways of conducting business. Some years ago I was visiting a well-known publisher in New York City to discuss a book project. The editorial offices were quiet. The carpets were thick. Conversations were carried on in hushed tones. The senior editor wore a conservative, three-piece suit. There was an air of Old World politeness. During the course of our conversation, I mentioned a directory that we were hoping to produce, utilizing a computer system. He suggested that I visit the directory division, a few blocks away. An hour later I entered an entirely different culture. Blue jeans were the norm. Ties were nowhere in sight. The people called to one another across low plywood partitions. There was no way of telling by the office layout who was in charge. As I walked in, the sense of drive and excitement was palpable.

In the editorial division, I had the feeling that if you didn't like the way things were going on, it might require a special meeting to discuss it with the senior editor, an appointment which no doubt had to be made through a secretary two weeks in advance. In the directory division I sensed that if people had a gripe, they walked up to whomever was responsible and, in rather confrontive terms, demanded to know, "What is going on here?" The former, hierarchical structure tends toward bureaucracy and rigidity and keeping one's cards close to the chest. In the latter there is an openness to discuss problems, not ignore them. In the former there is a tendency to want to climb the organizational ladder because that is where the perks lie. In the latter, there are few perks to covet.

A company's culture plays a large role in determining what is expected of employees and how success is defined or interpreted. There may be two different companies, each with exemplary standards, but one may provide a culture much more suited to an individual's personality, goals, and needs. It's important that cultures are not immediately painted as black or white.[3]

It is sometimes difficult to distinguish between a difference in values and a difference in style. During my early years as an engineering section head at Sperry Gyroscope, the company culture was "Tell it like it is." During a design review of a new product representatives of engineering, manufacturing, and sales would gather around a large layout drawing of the product. The conversation would move along something like this:

"How can you possibly like that? It's terrible!"

"Hey, bonehead, you know it worked well the last time we did it that way! Use your brains!"

"Come on, who in their right mind would ever design something like that?"

And so on. No personal offense was intended and seldom was it taken, especially if you had been around a while. When I moved to Lear in Grand Rapids I assumed that everyone worked that New York way. When I attended my first design review as the vice-president's technical assistant, I said exactly what I thought. I blew four people away and quickly got dubbed that "wise guy" New Yorker.

Both Sperry and Lear had similar corporate values; their business ethics were exemplary. But their styles and culture were entirely different. (I think my temperament was much better suited to New York, but Grand Rapids taught me some marvelous lessons!)

The Size of the Business

It is probably not unfair to say that "succeeding" in a small business setting brings many more temptations to violate the biblical norms than working in a larger corporation. Small business executives don't have time to establish many rules. They are completely involved with "making it" today. Someday when things are more in hand they will get around to working out the rules. Or maybe they rejoice that they don't have any real rules because they resist the thought of ever becoming a "bureaucracy." So they play it by ear, which often means that they may be doing something that is inherently unethical and not know it: off-hand decisions about a person's future, a too-quick response to a vendor's offer that looks a bit shady, chalking up time spent on personal business as company time. Informality is used as an excuse for not being civil to people. What is supposed to be a joke is really ill manners.

In the large company a lot of people have to abide by the same rules and what happens in one office may be quite foreign to another department. Not defining the rules can easily engender apparent favoritism. The large corporation has to decide how it will do things, to adopt an ethical stance for the business, and to try to apply the rules uniformly. Since people differ in their understanding of right and wrong, the company policy has to define what is permissible and what is not; what is desirable and what is forbidden.

During my career in aerospace I worked for two large corporations. There were very few times when I felt the need for challenging the business decisions of the organization on the grounds of my Christian ethics. Interestingly, when I moved into the world of Christian parachurch organizations, which are much smaller than most secular companies,[3] to my dismay, I often discovered that apparently their ethics were much lower than those of business! As I have analyzed some of the reasons for this, I've concluded that secular business executives, particularly those in large corporation, believe very strongly in the sinfulness of people and therefore set up rules and policies to keep people from sinning. The Christian organization, on the other hand, often assumes that because everyone is Christian, sin will not rear its ugly head. Wrong!

How the Business Is Organized

How the business is organized also has an impact on how people think of themselves and evaluate their personal success. In the past, most businesses were organized along a hierarchical, machinelike model. In such organizations the various components or positions are identified according to functions and required skills. An attempt is then made to find people who have the skills and willingness to carry out those functions. Hierarchies tend to screen out people whose gifts lie in the areas of generosity and compassion and mercy. Since the emphasis is on performance, it is assumed that people "want to get ahead," even though they are quite comfortable in their current position. Concepts such as "career track" imply that one needs to "move up" in the organization.

Fortunately, in recent years we have seen more and more organizations moving away from the hierarchical/military model to other images of an organization (Morgan, 1986). The biblical "biological" model of Ephesians 4 and 1 Corinthians 12 (one body, many parts) is one that seems to be gaining favor, even though today's organizational designers may have never read the New Testament.

Organizations that are designed along the hierarchical/military model tend to be closed, not significantly influenced by the outside environment, even within their industry. On the other hand, organizations which view themselves as open systems tend to relate to the outside. In business terms they are much more customer-oriented, and therefore much more responsive to listening to what the customer has to say in terms of the nature of the product or the service, its quality, timeliness, usefulness. This in turn impacts on the company's ethics and their concern for people, which is what ethics is all about.

Art and Glenn are engineers in a large hierarchical company. They are five levels down from the president. There are vice-presidents, division managers, department heads, and section heads. It is a long way up the ladder. Art and Glenn are responsible for the design of a new activator for the line of washing machines. They have been working on this design for almost a year and now they are in the midst of performing reliability tests. The word keeps coming down from above that the new activator is needed immediately to get the product line into stores well before Christmas. But the tests aren't going well. They talk to their engineering supervisor. Word is passed to the department head, but the report is not received warmly. "Get it done!" is the only reply. Glenn and Art talk it over. The activator has passed most of the tests, but not the durability tests. It will take at least a month of accelerated testing before usable results are available. Maybe the tests can be completed before manufacturing starts. Glenn and Art wish they could openly discuss this, but they can't. The "company" doesn't want to delay production. So the newly designed activator is released for manufacture. And Art and Glenn feel lousy.

The company defined success in terms of people meeting profit-oriented goals. It valued internal schedules more than engineering excellence and reliability. It imposed top-down instructions over bottom-up participation.

The Industry

The way businesses operate varies greatly from industry to industry. Established industries tend to have older organizational models, more rules and be less susceptible to change. Newer industries, such as electronic data processing, tend to have different cultures and a different mind-set about how they go about things.

Product organizations tend to focus on making a better, more profitable product, which usually means making one that has a high sales potential. Service organizations, on the other hand, are quickly impacted by the needs of those whom they serve, how close they are to the customer, and how fast the need for the service may change within the society. How a business views its customers will impact its ethics. A company that has a high commitment to its customers and takes a great deal of pride in meeting customers' needs will tend to value people and its employees. On the other hand, a company that is at a distance from any real customer can easily lose its concern for people in general (Peters and Waterman 1982).

Are there companies or industries for which a Christian should not work? Certainly. Sometimes this is obvious, sometimes much more opaque.

Some years ago we invited a young couple in the Sunday school class we taught to have dinner with us. We knew that they had been having a difficult time financially and that he was struggling in his job. In the course of the conversation it came out that the printing company he was working for was also printing pornographic literature. What did I think he should do? He wasn't directly involved with the pornography himself. "Quit!" I told him. "You have no business there." He knew that, but his friends had been telling him to take a wait-and-see approach before he left. The consequences of his quitting were not easy. He found it very difficult to get as good a job. Eventually the couple had to move out of state so he could find work. A tough decision, but a right one.

There are also much muddier waters. My first major job was with Sperry Gyroscope, then based solely in Lake Success, New York. Over 25,000 people were housed in a mile-long plant that made all kinds of sophisticated electronic gear, much of it for the military. I had a close Christian friend who was a pacifist and could not understand how I could work for such a company, even though I was working on commercial flight instruments. He worked for Long Island Lighting. My reply to him was a little too glib. "How can you work for a company that supplies power to a company that makes armaments?" But that's the kind of dilemma Christians often face.

Professionals

There is one group that is very much "in business" but is usually forgotten in a discussion like this. And yet they face more ethical decisions daily than many of us face in a year. They are the "professionals," particularly lawyers, doctors, accountants, consultants—men and women who are likely to be in business for themselves but who are expected to make decisions or give opinions about human behavior on a regular basis. Aside from the American Bar Association or the American Medical Association, they have little regular guidance that might help them become aware that some time ago they may have taken a wrong turn with long-term consequences.

How much should a doctor charge? If someone needs some simple advice over the telephone, should the doctor insist that the patient make an office visit? What about the ethics of doing lab tests in the doctor's office and charging what the traffic will bear? What about bilateral arrangements with laboratories or other medical service groups, arrangements which insure the doctor gets remuneration for the referral? None of these things are necessarily illegal. No one will naysay the decisions. Where does the guidance come from? Where is the gyroscope that keeps such professionals on an ethical course?

Why Do People Work?

This chapter began by noting that business offers us a personal identity, prestige, possessions, and power.

Before leaving this discussion on business it is helpful to ask again why people work. The obvious answer, "To make a living, to get ahead." We need to do our fair share, to provide for ourselves and others for whom we are responsible. The apostle Paul tells us quite sternly that everyone is supposed to work and support himself or herself (1 Thess. 3:10). The biblical idea behind work is to nurture and care for God's world and to provide for one another. Work should therefore be a fundamentally rewarding activity. At the end of his creation work, God took satisfaction in what he had done. "God saw all that he had made, and it was very good" (Gen. 1:31). To not enjoy the work we are doing is to be robbed of a basic dimension of human life.

So work has two ideal sides. On the one hand, there is the demand that we be responsible members of society. On the other hand, there is the reward that comes from seeing the results of our contribution to that society. The vast majority of Americans don't think about work so positively. Some years ago Studs Terkel interviewed hundreds of working Americans about their jobs. In his book *Working* (1985) we hear their voices. Few like work. Few enjoy it. Most see it as an evil necessity and feel devalued by work.

There are some significant changes taking place in American business's understanding of why people work. But we have a long way to go before we overcome some of the human deprivation caused by the Industrial Revolution. We will have more to say about that in chapter 4.

As we saw in chapter 1, we work because of (or in spite of) the fact that our jobs give us a sense of identity. The second question we ask a new acquaintance after learning his or her name is, "What do you *do*?" We put labels on others and ourselves according to our business or profession. This shouldn't be a surprise, nor is it a negative. Work takes up more time than anything else we do. That identity can be exhilarating or discouraging. Most people don't find much pride in doing the same thing day after day on an assembly line, but as we will see later, other factors are involved.

Unfortunately, our society sees some jobs as more valuable than others. Some years ago I was writing a book in which I said that in God's sight a plumber was just as important as a pastor. I believed that. I still do. But a good friend who reviewed the manuscript wrote in the margin, "I can't buy this." I suspect that's probably true of most Christians. They don't buy it either. It has to be more spiritual to be a pastor, doesn't it? Or does it?

We Work for Power

Another reason why people work is to gain *power*, power for good or power for bad, power for ourselves or power for the good of others. To work more effectively, we willingly give over the governance of our work to leaders. We recognize that part of work is planning, organizing, leading, and evaluating, and that this kind of "management work" is needed.[4] But that very concept creates the need for positions of authority in a business setting. The more authority we gain, the more influence we can have on decisions. The self-satisfaction we may find in such power can easily lead us toward acquiring more power for the very sake of having it.

"Power" is a slippery idea and is defined by each individual. There is power to tell others what to do, power to make one's own choices, power to affect the stream of events, power to have our own way, power to do something such as heal. The biblical understanding of power is divided between a Greek word that means authority (*exousia*) and one that means energy (*dunamis*) from which we get our own word *dynamite*. In our humanness we want both. We want authority to tell others what to do, and business can give us that. We want strength, energy, and resources, and business can offer us these. No wonder so many of us find it so satisfying! No wonder we are sometimes willing to buy into its standards at the expense of our own!

We Work for Prestige

This concept is closely related to working for power. Since in our society we do rate people according to their jobs, we naturally would like to have a job that gives greater recognition. People with titles like "Doctor," "Reverend," "Professor" or "President" seem to be a cut above the rest of us, and some of them are. People who have accomplished something and are well known have an aura about them. One man earns $30,000 a year shaping the lives of high school students. Another earns $2,000,000 a year because he can hit a baseball well. One woman makes $35,000 as a nurse. Lives are made whole because of her skills. Another woman makes $1,000,000 a year as a pop singer. Crazy. But true.

We Work to Make Money

Many people would equate working for a living with "making money." The more money we have, the more flexibility we have to make choices about how we will live, where we will live, what we will buy. The turn-of-the-century phrase "to make your fortune" embodies the idea that one should have a fortune (a sum of money much greater than what most others have). Money supposedly gives us more freedom to make choices. Here again we let the world define freedom for us. Later on we'll be talking about what it means to have "freedom in Christ" (James 1:25; 2:12). We will also talk more about money.

We Work for Fun

A final word about why we work. I hope *you* work because it is fun, not Disneyland kind of fun, but the kind we experience when we are with a group of friends and enjoying ourselves and someone says, "Hey, this is fun!" Or the kind of fun we are talking about when we do well at some sport and tell our coach, "That was fun!"

Life is not the proverbial bowl of cherries. It's tough. Success is not a feeling that comes from winning a one-sided game of golf with a novice or beating your ten-year-old at chess. There are mountains to climb, valleys to cross. There are times when all you worked for goes down the tubes. But if in balance you don't enjoy your job, quit it! If you are struggling to make ends meet as you read this page, that may seem like hollow counsel. I can only respond that if you are a Christian living in America, there are almost limitless opportunities open to you. As you set your face to lead a life that is pleasing to God I believe you will discover a "fun" job waiting for you.

Redefining Business?

Defining business and examining its impact on us has turned out to be much more difficult than you might have thought. You probably see that there won't be one set of rules that fits any business situation. Being "successful" in business *as a Christian* will depend on a variety of factors. Sometimes reconciling Christian ethics with your work is as simple as changing companies or industries. Other times it may require a confrontation with yourself or employer.

There will be more to say about how today's American business has evolved to where it is today. Perhaps the most important thing to understand is that the vast majority of today's American businesses define themselves in terms of profit, "the bottom line." This definition shapes their practices and, in the process, their ethics. On a more positive note, a growing number of businesses have concluded that a good bottom line is not enough. They are seeing that people *are* more important than anything else.

Wrapped up in our understanding of business is our understanding of why we work. That may take a lot of self-probing.

Reflections

In the previous chapter we talked about the many ways in which our definitions of "success" are made for us by others. What we have emphasized in this chapter is that the business we're in, the place where we spend most of our waking hours, also plays a major role in defining success for us. Before we move on and try to understand what we mean by "faith," it might be helpful for you to do some reflecting on what we have said.

1. How large is the business for which you are working?
2. How long have you worked there?
3. How much influence do you have on the decisions that it makes?
4. Is your business considered a leader in its field?
5. What impact is the industry of which your business is a part having on the way it makes decisions?
6. Would you consider that your business is most interested in profit as a bottom line or is it interested in some other results?
7. What do the answers to these questions tell you about your chances of "success" as it is measured by the business of which you are a part?

8. Why do you think *you* work? What is the most important reason? Is it fun?

9. If you are working through this book in a group setting (or if you have a friend whose judgment you trust), ask if they think this is the best job for you. If so, why? If not, why not?

Faith is not just something to believe. It is a story to be lived. From your individual viewpoint it is your story. But it is a story that needs to be written in light of the good news of Christ's story.

In the modern world we easily separate what we believe from what we do. We may be willing to agree that what we do is an evidence of our faith, but we describe the foundation of our faith by what we believe. However, the biblical idea of faith is that to say something is to do something.

Because biblical faith looks to God's Word to define how we should live, it gives us rules to live by that are based on unchanging truths. Reaching maturity is the result of constantly testing our faith and discovering that what we believe matches our experience in our home, in our church, in our business.

"And without faith it is impossible to please God, because anyone who comes to him must believe that he exists and that he rewards those who earnestly seek him" (Heb. 11:6).

3

What Is Faith?

Most mature Christians think of their faith as an ongoing pilgrimage of coming to know Jesus and learning what it means to follow him. For some of us it started with a set of firm beliefs, things we concluded must be true. For others including myself, it began with an experience that made a profound impression on them and started them on a new course. Some see faith as a statement of affirmations, such as the Apostle's Creed. Or it may be our perception of ourselves as church members. For many of us it began in our adolescent or teenage years. For some of us it is a journey we began as adults. If we sat down to write our own personal statement of faith, most of us would spend hours trying to make sure that we had all the different pieces together. We would not only want to state what we believe, but we would also want to give testimony to how those beliefs have worked themselves out in our lives. On the one hand, our faith is very complex and it has a lot of history. On the other hand, it is beautifully simple: God said it. I believe it.

A Story to Be Lived

Faith is not just something to believe. It is a story to be lived. For those of us just starting out on this wonderful adventure, it is a picture of what we would like to be, how we would like to see our lives develop. For those of us at the middle of life, it is a story of what has been and what we would yet want it to be. For those of us in the autumn time, it may be a remarkable account of a life well lived. Or perhaps it is a more somber story, filled with I-wish-it-might-have-beens.

From each individual's viewpoints it is "my story." It is what has happened to *me* or what *I* yet wish will happen. But there is more to it than that. Because my story needs to be written in light of the good news of Christ's story, faith merges these two stories into our story.

What is your story? How would you tell it? Perhaps you have played the Lifeline Game of picturing your life story as a graph drawn across a page. The horizontal line represents time. The vertical line represents happiness or a sense of well being, success, or failure. As you record the ups and downs of your story, the line goes up for positive, affirming times, and goes down for negative, in-the-depths experiences. The graph gives you an opportunity to talk about the story you have been living out. You might describe your graph as a measure of your faith: When were you close to God? When did things seem dry and the Lord far away? But that graph can only depict the past. What of the future? What will the graph look like in the days ahead?

To have faith is to be a storyteller. To grow in faith is to look back on that unrolling carpet of the past and find assurance that God was there. That story is told not only by our words but also by how we live. The world should be reading that story and asking, "What's going on here? Why does your life tell this story?" In *The Gospel in a Pluralist Society* (1986), Lesslie Newbigin suggests that biblical evangelism should be an answer given to such a question. The world should see something happening and ask, "Why is this happening? What does it mean?" What are we to say about our faith if the world never asks us about its results?

And the world *will* ask. One of the most startling things about the televangelist scandals of the 1980s was that few Christians realized that the world was applying entirely different standards to Jimmy Swaggart and Jim Bakker than it would to non-Christians. The world doesn't care if you have an extramarital affair. It's the norm. Watch any TV soap opera. But the world knows that *Christians* are not supposed to have sex outside of marriage, that Christians are supposed to be honest, that Christians are supposed to turn the other cheek, and to be more concerned for others than themselves. It's the Christians who set the standards by which the world judges us! So the world watches, and if your story is different, the world will ask why.

Faith Brings Hope

Implicit in faith is the idea of hope. As the writer to the Hebrews tells us, "Faith is the substance of things hoped for, the evidence of things not seen" (Heb 11:1 KJV). Entering into faith is entering into the expectation of a better future, a better story, not only in eternity, but also in this life. There is an assumption that "growing in grace" will mean a more rewarding, more satisfying life. The overwhelming joy of the new Christian is summed up in the Campus Crusade slogan of some years ago, "I FOUND IT!" In his parables Jesus compared it to the delight of finding a lost coin, the elation of finding a treasure in the field, the joy that prompts one to sell all to purchase one marvelous pearl (Luke 15:8–9; Matt. 13:44–45). Faith brings the assurance that good things are going to happen!

Faith is initiated by God and sustained by the work of the Holy Spirit. At the same time faith implies an ongoing cooperation with the work of that Spirit. The Spirit moves, but we are expected to move also. We are elected, chosen of God as his people, but the evidence of that selection is revealed in our daily·lives. What if our lives seem to reflect little faith? Is it possible to lose our salvation? Many Christians would answer yes; others would disagree. But those who disagree that salvation once obtained cannot be lost, often will quickly retreat to the position that a failed life is probably evidence that election was never made. We say with the apostle Paul, "Therefore, my dear friends, as you have always obeyed—not only in my presence, but now much more in my absence—continue to work out your salvation with fear and trembling" (Phil. 2:12).

The Absolute Absolute

Faith believes something that is true. Something that is true is something that does not change. It was certain yesterday, it is a fact today, it will be true tomorrow. Sometimes we emphasize that idea by saying, "That is *absolutely* true." An absolute can't be changed. The pluralism in our society, which we will discuss further along, has taken a turn that causes a lot of trouble with absolutes. In his book *What Americans Believe* (1991), researcher George Barna reports that on the average only 16 percent of Americans strongly believe in absolute truth. Perhaps more startling is the fact that among those who attend an evangelical church, only 27 percent believe in absolute truth.

My friend Sam Kamaleson is a pastor, teacher, evangelist, and a world-renowned conference speaker. Sam learned long ago that the primary basis for all faith is a belief in absolutes. He makes the point that all absolutes are God-given by calling God our "Absolute Absolute." He stands over every other absolute because he is the source and cause of them all. This is God's world. He created it. He created the way it works. He does not change. Neither does the way he works.

Translating Belief into Action

In the modern world we easily separate what we believe from what we do. The secular world does it, but Christians also do it. We agree that what we do is an evidence of our faith, but we define our faith according to what we believe. However, the biblical idea of faith is wrapped up in the Hebrew concept that saying something is doing something. Word and action are intimately related. Biblical faith says that to believe in justice is to be just. To believe in righteousness is to be righteous. To believe that one should be merciful is to be merciful. To believe in "Love your neighbor as yourself" is to love our neighbor unconditionally. "If anyone has material possessions and sees his brother in need but has no pity on him, how can the love of God be in him? Dear children, let us not love with words or tongue but with actions and in truth" (1 John 3:17–18).

Because biblical faith looks to God's Word to define how we should live, it provides us with a set of principles that are to result in a series of behaviors, rules to live by in different situations. These rules will vary between cultures, but there is the assumption that they apply to *all* of life in that culture. For example, "honesty" may work itself out differently in different societies and cultures. What might be considered as a bribe in one country may be considered part of normal business in another part of the world. But, in America, the idea that we have to pay someone to do what we believe they are supposed to do stands outside our understanding of good rules. (But let's not forget that many other "modern" societies think the practice of tipping is completely wrong since people should give good service if that's their job!)

The rules we live by have varied over the centuries. The Old and New Testament worlds within which God's revelation was given faced their specific set of problems and needs. Too often we look to the Bible for a set of explicit rules that can apply to a given situation. In most cases those rules are not there. Instead we find the basic *principles* of love, goodness, righteousness, mercy, and justice. From these principles and from the stories of the lives of the saints who have gone before us, we need to work out "with fear and trembling" those rules by which we will govern our lives.

Life is a daily testing of what we believe against what we are experiencing. Children have a very inaccurate view of the world and certainly an exalted view of the powerful people who are their parents. As we grow older, our experience teaches us certain things that we come to believe as "facts." Facts are things that we assume everybody believes. Gravity is a fact. There may be a few people in the world who don't believe in it, but from our viewpoint that is ridiculous. Hunger is a fact. As far as we can tell, all human beings become hungry if they do not eat. So it is with the need for oxygen. It is a fact that without it we will die. Facts, then, are truths which our society has agreed are beliefs everyone holds, or should hold if they are sensible and informed.

Faith goes beyond facts. It is the internal "evidence of things not seen." In that respect, faith is not "scientific." We cannot perform a series of repeatable experiments that will "prove the existence of God." True, we may see all kinds of evidence around us which testifies to his existence. We may say with the psalmist that "The heavens declare the glory of God and the firmament shows his handiwork" (Ps. 19:1 KJV). But in our world not everyone sees the same evidences for a Creator. So perhaps without realizing it, we put our facts and our faith on the line. What we claim to be the fact of God, the world will say is our *belief*.

Reaching spiritual maturity is the result of constantly testing our faith and discovering that what we believe matches our experience. When we talk about being a witness or giving a testimony, we mean showing others what we have experienced, telling our story. This sharing of experience is part of our Christian growth. When we find our place in a community of believers, we realize that we have a common set of beliefs, a set of propositions that are the basis of the way we act out our lives. If we have nothing to share, if we find no excitement in testing the reality of these propositions in everyday life, then they remain a set of things that "we believe," but which may have little to do with life as we live it.

This is one of the reasons it is important to be an integral part of a community of believers who have agreed on the rules it will live by and will encourage each other in that direction. Years ago, when we moved to Grand Rapids, we found an entirely different kind of Christian community—a far cry from what we had experienced in New York. Early on we discovered that "good Christians" didn't dance. This was a new idea to us. My wife and I had both gone to dancing school. We had met at the Cinderella Ball in New York when we were both fifteen. But during the five years we were in Grand Rapids, we never set foot on a dance floor. We accepted the fact that these new friends had decided from their interpretation of Scripture that they should not dance. Even though that was not part of our history, we accepted the norms of our new church. It was not always easy. A few months after joining Lear I was asked to organize the annual engineering dance. I had to explain that although I had no personal problem with dancing, I was a member of a fellowship that felt it was inappropriate, and therefore could not accept the assignment. The rules aren't universal. They are local. But if we live in community, they are still the norms we need to live by.

Testing Our Faith in the Workplace

In the world of business we encounter a whole range of other beliefs, other faith systems, generally based on "enlightened self-interest." We normally find it is in our best interest to worry about others' best interest. This is the secular equivalent of the Golden Rule, "Love your neighbor as yourself," except the basis for that is eventually selfishness rather than obedience. There is a wide range of understanding as to what that rule involves and whether indeed it works. At one end is the cynic who believes that the only way to survive is to look out for Number One. At the other end is the humanist who accepts a moral responsibility to look to the interests of others.

What rules do Christians follow? Do we go with the rules of the business, about which we may not be able to do anything? Is it possible to bring a biblically based set of rules to our job, rules that will help us to navigate through our everyday decisions? Is it as easy (or hard) as saying I can't go to the dance?

As Christians we have a vision of how God would have us live. But the world has a different vision. Each time we move into the world of business we are faced with other visions of what we should do, how we should act, how we should live. How we respond to these pressures greatly impacts our spiritual growth.

In my first full-time job as an engineer for Sperry Gyroscope we worked on government contracts. The government's rules for expense accounts stated that a daily meal allowance of $6.00 a day was all that would be allowed. However, the company recognized that it was very difficult for most people to eat on $6.00 a day, even in 1948. The solution was to tell the business traveler to put down $6.00 on the expense account and then add any meal expenses that were over and above that amount to some other innocuous and unverifiable expense, such as taxis. A small dilemma? A very real one! The company was trying to act in the best interest of its employees. It assumed that the government policies were unrealistic. My acceptance of the company's decision opened up a whole series of other questions later on when I became responsible for the actions of others.

To give another illustration, suppose the company's policy is that people are reimbursed for meals but not alcoholic beverages, and further suppose that an employee's normal practice is to have a glass of wine with dinner. Should the supervisor instruct the employee to ignore the company policy and just add the cost of the wine to the meal expense account?

What about keeping company hours? Most hourly employees work a forty-hour week but are allowed break times and have set meal hours. Is it wrong to stretch a ten-minute break to twenty minutes? If you are being paid $10.00 an hour, are you *stealing* from the company the $1.66 that extra ten minutes represents?

Some companies contract work and must account for what is known as "billable hours." The people working on a particular customer's job keep track of the hours spent on a job and bill the customer accordingly. Often the company has contracted with a customer to do a job for so many billable hours. What happens when the job is completed ahead of time? Suppose the customer was told the job would take ten hours, and it takes only seven. And suppose further that it is the company policy to bill the customer for the hours quoted, even though the work did not take that long. What are the implications?

Your company is bidding against others for a particular job. How quickly the job can be completed will be a major factor in the decision as to who gets the job. You estimate that the job will take forty days.

Your supervisor says, "We need the business. Tell them we'll get it done in a month." What do you do?

Myriads of these seemingly small decisions shape our view of what is acceptable and what is not. "Learning the business" turns out to be not just the technical side of finance, real estate, engineering, construction, hotel management, or what have you. Those details are wrapped up in what is essentially a world view of not only what works but what is right and what is wrong.

"Thou shalt not lie." Is underquoting the job a lie?

"Thou shalt not steal." Is taking an unauthorized twenty-minute break stealing from the company?

"Thou shalt not bear false witness." Is following the supervisor's instruction to pad the number of hours on the bill bearing false witness?

Small decisions snowball into decisions so large that we can no longer ignore the contrast with what we say we believe. A manager tells inspectors to falsify inspection records and an airplane crashes and people are killed. An aircraft executive's drive for more business leads him to pay a middleman to help obtain a foreign-government contract, and a national scandal ensues. It all happens so subtly. The small decisions at the beginning of our business careers are the seeds of larger decisions farther down the line. And one day we awaken to the reality that what we are hearing and saying in church, or even teaching to a Sunday school class of young people, is not the story we are acting out in the everyday world. Faith has become reduced to a set of propositions. What we say on Sunday has become divorced from Monday's performance.

The tragedy is how easy it seems to lead two lives (or three or four). As we will see in later chapters, our society has shaped us to play a number of roles, to lead different lives. We use different language in some situations than we do in others. We emphasize certain facts with one audience but not with another. Even more tragically, we decide that this is what the normal Christian life is all about. It isn't.

Reflections

1. What are the absolute truths in your life?
2. Think about your last few weeks at work. What happened in your life there that you feel doesn't jibe with Christian ethics?
3. What things happened in your company that didn't square with the Ten Commandments or the Sermon on the Mount?
4. What is going on in your industry that might not be happening if Jesus was setting the rules?
5. To what extent is your business life different from your "Christian" life? Why do you think this is so?
6. What does your performance at work tell you about your faith? Are you applying the same values on the job as elsewhere in your life?
7. As others share their answers with you, what do *their* answers tell you about your own situation?

Part 2

The Setting for the Story

Money is a vehicle of exchange that has come to have a value in itself. Without it society as we know it could not exist. Most of us believe that having money gives us freedom of choice. How did money evolve?

The Industrial Revolution and the Enlightenment have produced the kind of world we live in, a world that holds rational thought and science as the arbitrators of all we believe. How did that happen?

Our industrialized, capitalist, modern society by its nature tends to divide and segment each of us into a number of different persons. Because we play many different roles, we miss the wholeness of life, and our Christianity seems but another role. If we can see how this came about, we can take steps to integrate our Christian life into all of life.

4

Today's Workplace

As we probe deeper into our examination of the major pieces of our dilemma—success, business, and faith—we realize that we want and need a better understanding of the battle in which we are engaged and the ground on which it is being fought. The workplace was not always as it is today. Modern business is dramatically different from the workplaces of our forebearers. If we can see how business and the workplace evolved from simple beginnings, we can better understand who we are as business people and why we think and act as we do. Then perhaps we can better resist the world's attempt to shape us into its mold and change that world for the better. The struggle to find our own God-given understanding of success is not new. It is a battle that has been fought by the saints through the ages. But each era brings new situations that need to be faced by the church and by individual Christians. Culture is always changing, and in recent years changes have come at an ever-increasing pace. Without our knowing it, culture fits us with a pair of distorted lenses through which we view our world, and as a consequence events sneak up on us when we least expect them.

Cultural Astigmatism

Because we are shaped by forces we seldom understand, we tend to attempt to understand our world in terms of our immediate environment. We don't think much about what's happening in Timbuktu or London or Calcutta, or even another American city. All human beings think that way. Each society sees the world through its own cultural lens. The same is true of us as individuals. We try to make sense out of the world we face in terms of our own experience. When the time comes to make a major decision, one that is much more far-reaching than anything else we have experienced, we fall back on what we personally believe.

Unfortunately, the larger problems of life are not simple extensions of smaller ones. But we tend to think they are. The only experience we have is our own experience and that of others around us. So we take that experience and use it as best we can. At the moment you are faced with a very important question: "How can you succeed in business without losing your faith?" If you look only at your own experience, you may never find the answer. You need to look at the experience of those who have gone before you and those who live alongside you.

Some years ago researchers at MIT put forth the notion of "counterintuitive thinking." Their research indicated that when we base our decisions about major dilemmas on the intuition of personal experience, we stand a good chance of being wrong. The way events work out on a small scale is not necessarily an indicator as to how they will work on a larger scale. The results are counter to what our developed intuition tells us. We can see how this might apply to our attempts to understand "the world," or a large enterprise like an industry. We need to look at the big picture and attempt to comprehend that, as difficult as that may be.

Richard Neustadt and Ernest May come at it from a different view. In their book *Thinking in Time* (1988), they analyze major decisions made in government during the past fifty years and conclude that few decisions were made in light of history. (This American penchant for valuing the present over the future will be discussed later.)

How did our society evolve? What can we learn from its history? Examining two major factors, the evolution of money and the Industrial Revolution, will help us understand not only how the workplace became what it is today, but also how an industrialized society tends to compartmentalize our lives and force us to play various roles. If we see the consequences of this role assignment on our understanding of success, we will be well on our way in our struggle to reconcile our Christian beliefs with our business practices.

Money

Today's society could not operate without money. It has become such a normal part of everyday life that it is the measure of all our possessions and the basis for understanding modern business. The exchange of one's possessions or energy for someone else's possessions or energies is involved in business. People who are naturally gifted in one area exchange their skills to obtain things that others already have. Robert is a skilled cabinet maker. Joshua is a capable shoemaker. Robert wants a pair of shoes. Joshua wants a new cabinet. The exchange medium of business is money.

Money was one of humanity's early inventions. Why so early? Well, suppose I wanted to exchange my cow for an attractive piece of jewelry and the jeweler lived ten miles away. It was no simple matter to exchange a cow for a piece of jewelry. But that was the way it had to be done. Then someone asked the question, "What is of common value to everyone but valuable enough so that it doesn't weigh too much to carry around?" The answers were many: shells, stones, ivory, furs, tobacco. From the earliest times precious metals, such as gold and silver, gained wide use. Coins were minted. As gold and silver were recognized for their beauty and scarcity, and thus of high value, a given amount of one of these metals was put into these government-minted-coins. When large amounts were needed, it was not uncommon to weigh out the coins. Hence the British description of one of their monetary units as a "pound," originally a pound of silver pennies. A sheepherder might measure his wealth by the number of sheep. Tradesmen or businessmen would measure wealth by the amount of money (coins shaped from precious metal) they had. Ingenious governments eventually thought of ways to make the exchange even simpler. A piece of paper printed by a government was issued (supposedly) for a given amount of silver or gold. Our American dollars used to have a statement on them identifying them as redeemable for silver. Today they are like letters of credit. When a government stands behind these pieces of paper, it is no longer necessary to exchange them for gold or silver because the government has guaranteed that one can get like value for them. (Of course, when governments print more money than they have assets for, the value of the paper declines, and the result is inflation.)

Money quickly took on a value of its own, not for what it was, but for what it represented. It could be counted, banked, talked about, and used as a measure of one's ability to obtain possessions. In so doing it took on a *life* of its own to the extent that the apostle Paul could say, "For the love of money is a root of all kinds of evil. Some people, eager for money, have wandered from the faith and pierced themselves with many griefs" (1 Tim. 6:10). In enumerating all the signs of the end days, Paul lumped the love of money with all kinds of evil: "People will be lovers of themselves, lovers of money, boastful, proud, abusive, disobedient to their parents, ungrateful, unholy, without love, unforgiving, slanderous, without self-control, brutal, not lovers of the good" (2 Tim. 3:2–3). That's a pretty heavy indictment!

Money was invented to make trading easier and without it modern business could not work. But money turned into a genie that we can't seem to keep in the bottle! Now we use it not only to measure business success, but also as a yardstick for personal success.

The Industrial Revolution and Its Effects

Although ancient kings and princes might have engaged in what today we call "big business," for thousands of years the vast majority of people carried out small businesses only in their local areas. As we read about the rebuilding of Jerusalem, we discover perfumers and jewelers and other trades allocated places around the city (Neh. 3:8). People in the same craft or trade naturally grouped together to learn from one another. There was a guild of silversmiths who made statues of Diana in Ephesus and whose business was threatened by Paul's announcement of a new faith in Jesus (Acts 19:23–27).

This state of affairs continued until the seventeenth century. The discovery of the New World had brought an influx of precious metals and other forms of wealth into Europe. The great distances involved required the establishment of a system of credits, which in turn promoted new ways of banking. The seventeenth century was notable for the Commercial Revolution as increases in wealth raised the demand for new products. During this same time Europe was gradually shifting from wood to coal as a primary fuel. Britain had an abundance of coal and iron, and the need to deal with these sources of power prompted a series of inventions. Thomas Newcome's steam engine in 1705 was designed to help lift coal from the pits and James Watt's improvements on it in 1764 forecast the modern steam engine. John Wilkinson's cannon-boring machine (1774) made it possible to produce strong cylinders, which made the steam engine more powerful and efficient. Meanwhile, the textile industry was undergoing major changes. John Kay's fly shuttle (1733), James Hargreaves' spinning jenny (patented 1770), Richard Arkwright's water frame (1769), Samuel Crompton's mule (1779), which combined the features of the jenny and the frame, and Edward Cartwright's power loom (patented 1783), all completely changed the way cloth was woven. In terms of the number of needed work hours, these innovations increased production a hundredfold. The Industrial Revolution was underway. Many people contend it was not a "revolution" because its changes spread well over one hundred years.

During this same period Henry Bessemer invented a new process for making steel. A clay-lined cauldron with small vents in the bottom was filled with iron ore and heated by coal. Air was blown up through the vents into the molten metal. The oxygen in the air combined with the various impurities to burn them into slag, further heating the metal. The result was a highly efficient conversion process that is used to this day. The cost of manufacturing steel dropped dramatically. The next logical development was the use of machines for making machines. Multiple machines could now be brought into one location and powered by one steam engine through a series of belts.

The Compartmentalization of Life

The Industrial Revolution replaced the guilds with factory businesses which brought a large number of workers under the same roof. The workplace was removed from the home. Rather than experiencing the ebb and flow of daily life surrounded by family and friends, what went on at the factory was separated from the rest of life. The compartmentalization of life, and a new way of thinking about one's self had begun. Since distances that people could and would travel to and from home to work were limited by transportation, people lived in communities. The neighborhood of family and friends continued to exist. The neighborhood and its values continued to exert an influence on how people behaved, on what was right and what was wrong. But during the day at the factory there was a different set of rules, rules that limited people's behavior and choices. There was one set of rules or values to be followed at home and another set to be followed at work. Since home and work were separated, it became normal to think of two ways of living one's life.

This is part of what we are experiencing today. We leave one world and enter another with a different set of values. At home love may be the supreme value. Many of us would gladly die for our spouse or children. At work "the bottom line" is often the supreme value, and too often we feel like we are being asked to die for it.

The Loss of Personal Skills

The Industrial Revolution had at its heart the division of labor into separate steps and the subsequent ability of machines to replace people for many of the steps. The resulting increase in productivity was an amazing phenomenon. It generated wealth for the owners of factories while at the same time it debased the inherent skills of the working person. As machines replaced hand tools, skilled artisans lost their place in life and their identity. As machines and new tools increased efficiency in agriculture, thousands of farm workers moved to the cities to find work in factories.

By the turn of the nineteenth century two factors had combined to further atomize individuals and the family. The first was the introduction of interchangeable parts, which permitted the production of a large number of identical items. Prior to the American Civil War every piece of a product was unique. Each bayonet was fitted to a particular rifle, whose internal parts had been fitted to one another. A wagon wheel was constructed for a particular wagon. Every cover was fitted to a matching pot. Once parts were standardized and there was no need for special fitting, costs were immensely reduced.

One can see the impact of interchangeable parts in our second reason why personal skills decreased in importance: Frederick Taylor's concept of "scientific management." Taylor was a self-made man with an inordinate need to bring order into his world. He imagined that if every task could be done with maximum efficiency, the waste of trial and error could be reduced. He started experimenting to discover the best way to adjust machine tools. Machinists were still using their own opinions as to what was best. Taylor set out to find the optimum and then have everyone do it the same way. This led to his analysis of how human beings work best. Starting with an analysis of the best way to shovel, he extended his experiments to every facet of every job in the factory. Jobs were broken down into the smallest possible component. Needed skills were reduced to a minimum by having each person repeat the same task over and over. People were fitted to jobs in a machinelike manner. The broad skills needed by the guild craftsmen were no longer needed. The identity that one may have had as an artisan was sacrificed for a higher pay (more money!). Another basic value was removed. The skilled craftsman was replaced by the (better paid) "blue collar" worker. Once everyone could be identified by their occupation. People called Carpenter, Smith, Farmer, Mason, and others had taken their very names from their occupation. They knew who they were. But what is a "blue collar worker"?

It does not require an understanding of the history of manufacturing to conclude that most workers didn't like this. Management was surprised. They thought that because individual wages were going up, and the country was producing more and more, workers would be happy. They were not. The needs of World War I pushed the ideas of "scientific management" throughout the country. In response the modern labor movement arose in defense of workers who saw themselves as devalued, victimized. Wages rose some more. Unions gained great concessions from business, but unhappiness remained. Why?

Enter the psychologists who explained that workers were unhappy because their personal needs for achievement were not being met. Management theorists such as Eldon Mayo, Chris Argyris, and Frederick Herzberg uncovered what motivated people and what demotivated them. Unfortunately, business used their findings to try to quiet unrest and paid little attention to the machinelike structures that the application of Taylor's theories produced. Decision making and action were kept separated. Even more importantly management started using psychological insight to manipulate people into *believing* that things were better. It didn't work.

In his milestone book, *The Practice of Management* (1954), Peter Drucker pointed out the reality of what he called in one chapter "Management by Objectives and Self-Control." Drucker realized that business had a goal—to make a profit—and that to try to make people believe otherwise was foolish. But Drucker also realized that individual, personalized goals *which workers help plan and for which they accept responsibility* are tremendous motivators. People are imaginative. They are creative. Give them an opportunity to help plan things and they will start suggesting changes, improvements. Put them together in working teams where they can form a social unit, and all kinds of good things will happen for both the workers and the company. People will broaden both their responsibilities and their work with one another. For an excellent discussion on this subject see Lee Hardy,

The Fabric of This World: Inquiries into Calling, Career Choice and the Design of Human Work (1990).

But the damage of the Industrial Revolution has already been done. We have all learned to play different roles. And in those different roles we have become adept at applying different values.

Capitalism

The innovative machines of the Industrial Revolution were too expensive for the average artisan to buy to replace his hand tools, which created the factory system and a new kind of capital formation. As machines increased agricultural efficiency, and more and more people were forced off their farms to work in the cities, wages were depressed. People with money to invest—capitalists—were in the saddle. Some of the resultant abuses included the use of child labor in factories and the uncontrolled accumulation of wealth. The then-current laws of society had not contemplated such situations. Britain did not institute child labor laws which covered all industries until 1833, even though it had already abolished slavery. The unbridled use of wealth produced the "robber barons" of Europe and the United States.

Capitalism enabled the development of large industries and the complex business systems we have today. But it also put the emphasis on the amount of wealth accumulated, rather than the goods produced. Built into the idea of capitalism is the notion of the most gain for the least amount of effort for the person with the capital. Such "free trade" has had to be continually reined in by governments to ensure the greater good of the people. Anti-trust laws, cigarette advertising restrictions, truth-in-lending laws, Social Security—all testify to the fact that "pure" capitalism works for the good of a few at the expense of the many. This is not to decry capitalism per se. As has often been remarked, it may not be the best social system, but in its controlled form it is the best we have discovered so far.

The Loss of Social Controls

The invention of the automobile and its rapid adoption through-out the United States in the twentieth century permitted a flexibility of lifestyle that quickly led to the demise of the extended family. In ear-lier years, grandmothers, grandfathers, cousins, and aunts and uncles were born, lived, and died in the same town. Everyone knew everyone else's business. The town had general agreement on what was per-missible and what was proper. People looked out for one another, and they generally adhered to the community norms because it would be very uncomfortable not to. It was unusual for someone to leave home "to make their fortune."

With the advent of the automobile and the growing network of railroads, people could leave the social controls of the village and town for the relative anonymity of the city. The few restraints that might have slowed the move to complete individualism had been removed. A person could create his or her own world. The city had dif-ferent norms than the town or village.

Those of us who travel for business have experienced this phe-nomenon. When away from family and friends, out of sight of anyone who knows us, temptations multiply. In our motel room may be pay-to-watch movies on TV, films we would never look at when home. Who is to know what we eat or drink, or what we do? Anonymity works against social controls, and history demonstrates all too well that with-out social controls each of us will do what seems right in our own eyes.

The Enlightenment

The Industrial Revolution came on the heels of a time when reli-gious values were being questioned throughout Europe and North America. This was the Age of the Enlightenment, the Age of Reason. The discoveries of Isaac Newton, the rationalism of René Descartes and Pierre Bayle, the pantheism of Benedict de Spinoza, the empiricism of Francis Bacon and John Locke fostered a belief in natural law and universal order and great confidence in human reason. Prior to the

Enlightenment Western civilization generally assumed that the Bible was the absolute basis of all truth. No longer. No longer were men and women seen as being made in the image of God. No longer was the revelation of Scripture considered normative for all people. A rational and scientific approach to religious, social, political, and economic issues promoted a secular view of the world, a general sense of progress, and confidence in man's ability to perfect himself. The proponents of the Enlightenment agreed on several basic attitudes. With supreme confidence in rational man, they sought to discover and act on the universally valid principles that supposedly governed nature, humanity, and society. They vigorously attacked spiritual and scientific authority, dogmaticism, intolerance, censorship, and economic and social restraints. Common values which were once held by the majority of people were now being challenged. Another compartmentalization was taking place, another anchor pulled up, another set of values destroyed.

The Roles We Play

The idea that we all play different roles in life is rather new. The concept obviously comes from the stage where an actor plays different roles for different performances. He or she acts out the lines that have been written by someone else. Shakespeare was ahead of our modern world. Long before we saw ourselves as playing different roles he summed it up with "all the world's a stage, and all the men and women merely players,"[1] and his gloomy "Life's but a walking shadow, a poor player that struts and frets his hour upon the stage and then is heard no more."[2] But Shakespeare, while well understanding the turmoil that goes on in the human breast, probably did not foresee the many roles we play, one after another, within the *same* character.

These role divisions are reinforced daily by our surrounding culture. At home we play the role of Child, Parent, Spouse, or all three. As we become Christians we take on a new role: Church Member. When we enter the workplace, many of us find a close association with our profession, whether it be Computer Programmer, Real Estate Agent, Doctor, or Flight Attendant. In trying to describe this play-acting in an essay some years ago, I said I felt like I had a rotary switch on the side of my neck. When I got in the car in the morning, I switched to Carpool Rider. At the office door, I turned the switch again, this time to Engineer. Sometime during the day I might have an opportunity to share a word about Christ with a fellow-worker, and I switched to Witness. As I got out of the car in front of my home in the evening, I kept my hand on the switch because I never knew who I was going to play—Father, Husband, or Lover!

Each of these roles has built-in expectations. We learn to shift very easily from one set to another. When we visit our parents, we know that a child is expected to act in a certain way, and we usually conform. When we enter the church building on Sunday, we shift gears to meet another set of expectations. Whereas in public places we may pay no attention to strangers, in church we are expected to welcome people we don't know. In public places we understand that we are supposed to take our turn or our place in line, and we become upset when others try to "break in." On the other hand, at home with our family we may think nothing of interrupting. (As Robert Frost said, "Home is the place where, when you have to go there, they have to take you in"!) Interestingly, we adapt to these different sets of rules so naturally that we don't even recognize that we might be working with different sets of ethical principles.

Many of our roles are hidden from others. A child asks a parent, "Mommy, what do you do at work?" because what mommy (or daddy) does and the rules under which she does it are quite strange to her children. They may also be completely unknown to her spouse. In the same way what we do at church, and the rules that we work with there, may be completely unknown to co-workers. They may know that we are "Christian," but that may have no meaning to them in terms of how they see us living out our lives.

As we play these many different roles, we wonder about our identity. Who am I, really? Am I the person my colleagues meet at work each morning? Am I the person who is teaching a Sunday school class each Sunday? Will the real me please stand up! This division into many different selves can leave us detached from reality. Much of the stress in modern society results from trying to keep up with the constantly changing demands of our different roles.

One can argue that human beings have always played different roles in life, even though the number of roles was much smaller. What one does as a fisherman, a father, a tribal leader are different. But what we have lost is a common set of values which controls our actions in all our roles. In an earlier day people had a strong sense of identity. No matter where they were, somehow they knew *who* they were. Not so today. Where do we find *universal values*?

Christians are not alone in asking this question. The search for significance is very much on our American minds. So we ask, Who am I? How am I different? How can I be *me*? What does it mean to be me?

When asked what was the greatest commandment, Jesus replied "You shall love your God with all your heart, with all your soul, with all your mind. This is the first and great commandment. The second is like it, you shall love your neighbor as yourself" (Matt. 22:37–39 KJV). The Law of Love is the ultimate law of God's kingdom, but the idea of one ultimate law for all of life repels not only the secular mind, but all too often the mind of the modern Christian. In his book titled *The Christian Mind* (1963), Harry Blamires argued that we no longer have categories in which to think "christianly." The many roles we play have robbed us of a general set of references. Our lives *have* been changed by the renewing our minds, but they have been changed in the wrong way. Instead of hanging on to our Christian understanding of reality, we have been forced to accept the world's categories, the world's language, the world's thought forms to describe what we mean, what we think.

We need to find our way back to a place where we are controlled by one mind—the mind of Christ.

Reflections

1. List the roles that are a daily part of your life. Are there rules in one role that have nothing to do with another? (If you are working with a group, combine your lists to make a composite picture.)

2 Is there a common set of rules that you apply to all of your roles? If not, why not?

3. How are the rules or values different at your business from what they are at home or church?

4. In what way do your various roles keep you from leading a Christian life?

5. What would have to happen for you to have the "mind of Christ" in all your roles?

6. Go back and look at the four descriptions you wrote at the end of chapter 1. Note particularly the one that described how you would like others to know you. What roles do you play in this one?

B usiness does not exist in a world by itself but in a society that has its own set of values. Families differ. Communities differ. Countries differ. To understand how to be a Christian in business without losing our faith we need to understand the origin and current impact of eight key American values.

Pluralism leads to the conviction that everyone has a right to his or her own belief.

Equality assumes we are all born equal.

Individualism counters the biblical basis of community.

Materialism equates possessions with success.

That in turn promotes competitiveness.

Capitalism defines the ground rules of business.

The notion that each generation is better than the last cuts us off from history and all we might learn from it.

American civil religion waters down our faith.

All these "American" values are potential roadblocks to an integration of faith.

5

Today's Society and Its Values

Obviously "business" does not exist in a world by itself. Although international business and multinational corporations are commonplace, the country and the society in which we work set many of the rules. As Lockheed Aircraft discovered some years ago, what was good business in Japan was considered bribery in the United States. Lockheed wanted a contract from the government of Japan. Arrangements were made to pay certain sums to an official in Japan to make this possible. The Japanese thought that was fine. The United States didn't. Lockheed was fined millions of dollars. One government sets rules which may differ from those of other countries. In the United States if your company has a government contract, it is subject to a host of rules about the kind of accounting it must do and the reports it must submit, as well as numbers of federal regulations that might not apply to a private contract. Such rules may be quite unknown in another industrialized country. A major task of a cross-cultural missionary is to understand the rules, the culture, of the host country, to put aside his or her own cultural (but not Christian!) values and see "reality" through new lenses.[1]

Each of our fifty states sets rules. For example, California has rules about who is be paid overtime after forty hours of work and who is not. Other states differ. In California if you ask a nonsalaried worker to work extra hours, you must pay overtime of time-and-a-half the regular hourly wage. If you don't, even though the employee does not protest, both you and the employee have violated the law.

In addition to these formalized regulations there are a host of unwritten laws that delineate acceptable and unacceptable behaviors. These rules are based on values that we generally hold as Americans. But values keep changing. As we saw in our brief history of the workplace, what was commonplace and accepted a hundred years ago may no longer be acceptable. And what was not acceptable ten years ago may now be acceptable. A good illustration of the latter is the movie rating system. In an effort to keep itself free from government regulation the movie industry created a series of ratings for films: G, PG, R, and X. These ratings were designed to inform the public, and parents in particular, of the nature of a movie so they could take personal responsibility for themselves or their children's attendance. If it's a G, don't worry. If it's PG, better give Parental Guidance. If it's R, it's Restricted and hopefully the theater won't admit children seventeen or under without an accompanying parent. If it's X, only adults are allowed to see it. Most of the ratings evaluated explicit sexual behaviors, use of vulgar language, and violence. But what was not acceptable to the general public ten years ago is evidently acceptable today. One has only to compare a PG movie of ten years ago with one today to discover that somewhere along the way values changed. Most of today's PG movies would have been rated R ten years ago. Now to replace X we have NC-17. Supposedly anyone under seventeen is not admitted. What a change in public values in a short time!

Variables in Our Value System

Every unit in society has its own set of values. Families have their sets of values and customs and what we call manners. I was taught as a child that when buttering a roll, one broke off a mouth-sized piece, buttered that piece and ate it before buttering another piece. As far as I was concerned what my parents had taught me as "good manners" was something everyone did or should do. I was shocked one day when one of my adult daughters cut her roll in two and buttered the half!

Families have rules about how often we touch base with each other, what language is acceptable in the home, what time children are expected to return from a date. We are aware that there are different rules in other homes, but usually we assume ours are best.

Communities, too, have values and customs, many of which are backed by laws. The Constitution and the Supreme Court have given local communities a great deal of latitude to govern themselves according to locally held values and social beliefs. Some communities have laws about the hours and days of operation of local businesses. Again, the majority of the people in each community assume they know what the rules ought to be.

Values and customs vary among social classes in America. Sociologists divide American society into upper/upper class, lower/upper class, upper/middle class, lower/middle class, upper/lower class, and lower/lower class. Each of these groups has a set of rules, with the lower/lower class holding a set far different from all the others. These values are the result of poverty and its accompanying insecurity. When you have no certainty that you will eat tomorrow, the "rules of society" have little meaning to you.

Values and customs vary widely among ethnic groups. Fifty years ago the United States was believed to be a melting pot. As new immigrants arrived, they were expected to learn English and be homogenized into the general society. We realize today that is not fully possible and American society is rapidly becoming a multiracial, multilingual mosaic. If there was ever any doubt about that, it was put to rest after the civil rights movement of the Sixties. Blacks affirmed their right to be *black* (Afro) Americans and to have their own culture.

We see the same phenomenon among other ethnic groups. There are more Spanish speakers in the United States than in some Latin American countries. The role of the male among Hispanics is quite different from his Anglo counterpart. Chinese, Koreans, Indians, Russians, and a host of other national groups have their own societies. On any given Sunday morning the Southern Baptists in Los Angeles preach in over thirty languages.

Superseding all of these values is a set of distinctive *American* values that have a major impact on how we think and what we do. Not everyone thinks the same, but certain principles have a major influence on our laws, our rules of conduct. These values shape our ideas of success, our ideas of what is appropriate (or inappropriate) in business and, in a very subtle way, our views of faith.

Eight "American" Values

Where did our so-called American values come from? How did they become so diverse and yet so strong? One might want to first ask, "What are these values?" But as we will see, analyzing their source helps us to understand what they are.[2] We will look at eight American values that particularly bear on our topic of "Succeeding in Business without Losing Your Faith." In looking at the development of each we will see not only how values are formed, but also what they are today and how they shape our attitudes and our actions.

Pluralism

Among modern nations the United States has a unique history. Unlike Europeans, Asians, and Africans our history had a very late beginning. The New World was what Europeans called it. A seemingly endless continent, separated from the rest of the world by two huge oceans and populated by less than 500,000 people, was suddenly discovered by the rest of the world. Although Spanish explorers had reached California in 1542, the first attempt at European settlement was at Jamestown, Virginia, in 1607. This commercial enterprise was a failure, but thirteen years later our "forefathers," the Pilgrims, landed near Plymouth Rock in what is now Massachusetts, and modern American history began. To understand the American character and value system, we need to begin there.

The Pilgrims left a social revolution behind them in Europe. For hundreds of years European thought and society had been dominated by religion. The church was the dominant authority, and even kings served at the pleasure of the Pope. The first major challenge to this authority came from Martin Luther at the beginning of the sixteenth century. Luther was followed by Calvin, and (for reasons quite other than theology) by Henry the Eighth of England, who wanted to be free of the Pope's control. The seventeenth century was dominated by the Enlightenment, as was discussed briefly in the last chapter. This movement centered on the idea that all the world needed to be subjected to rational analysis, that the human mind was the ultimate judge of what was fact and what was not. Religion, therefore, had to be rational, to be subject to the human mind's ability to grasp and explain it.

The Pilgrims left the seedbed of this new kind of thinking to find "religious freedom," by which they meant the freedom to believe what they thought was right and to establish a society based on those beliefs. The Mayflower Compact committed these early settlers to a uniform set of rules and beliefs as a community. But they faced an immediate problem. Just as they left their homeland because of their beliefs, so other emigrants did the same but arrived with different views, particularly as to the relationship between church and state. Thus Roger Williams was banned from the Massachusetts Bay Colony in 1631 and founded a new community—what is now Rhode Island. Others followed in different directions. Instead of the monolithic Christian society of the Pilgrims' dreams, the New World rapidly became pluralistic. It became accepted that you were not compelled to think like I do, worship like I do, even believe in God as I do. "Freedom" meant it was OK to be and do what I wanted, as long as I didn't violate the larger standards of law or commonly held beliefs about decency.

This is an important point. Pluralism is so imbedded in "the American way" that we assume it is the most sensible approach to building a society. As we try to shape our lives or influence our workplace, pluralism works both for and against us. It makes it "acceptable" to have ideas that are different from our co-workers', even as they feel no compulsion to accept (or reject) my ideas. They view them as my ideas, not theirs.

Today pluralism is a key American value. In fact, the only strong value most Americans hold is the right of everyone to hold his or her own values! Nothing wrong with that, but it leads to all kinds of implications for us as Christians and as business people. It evolves into such philosophies as, "It's all right to do this if no one gets hurt." It scoffs at the idea that any one person's ideas can be right and another's wrong. It thinks of Christianity (and any religion) as a set of beliefs, not facts: "You have a right to hold these beliefs, and a right to attempt to convince me of their validity, but you have no right to hold me accountable to standards of behavior based on those beliefs." This was not too bad when we thought of Americans as predominantly of European extraction, divided among Protestants and Catholics and a few Jews, but all sharing a common Judeo-Christian heritage. Today we have a multiplicity of imported and homegrown religions, each with its own understanding of proper conduct.

Equality

The settlers continued to arrive in the New World from all over Europe, bringing their cultures with them. What is now New York City was New Amsterdam, just as there was a *New* England, a *New* Brunswick, *New* Hampshire, *New* Jersey, *New* London (on the Thames River!), and *New* Sweden.

They came without servants. Today we would say they "had to make it on their own." The absence of servants and the need to depend on oneself and one's neighbors rapidly destroyed any Old World class consciousness that might have crossed the Atlantic with them. *Equality was an early American value.*

The Declaration of Independence didn't call equality a *religious* value. The Founding Fathers covered that by saying that it is "self-evident" that all men are created equal. But equality *is* a Christian value. Every person stands equal before God. All have sinned, all stand

under judgment (Rom. 3:23). All are also exposed to his uncondi-
tional love. Christians are people who acknowledge their sinfulness
and put their faith in the death and resurrection of Jesus Christ to be
put right with God. For Christian and non-Christian alike, equality is
an encouraging idea. It helps us to believe that anyone can make it
in America.

Individualism

Equality in a pluralistic society permitted individuals to see themselves as separate from any restrictions of society, free to choose their
religion and abiding place. If they didn't like the rules of one community, they could move farther away and set their own rules. The
result was the unique attribute of Americans—*individualism*. Writing
in 1831, the French historian Alexis de Tocqueville described individualism as he observed it in America this way:

> *Individualism* is a novel expression, to which a novel idea has given
> birth. Our [European] fathers were only acquainted with *egotism* (self-
> ishness). Selfishness is a passionate and exaggerated love of self, which
> leads a man to connect everything in the world. Individualism is a
> mature and calm feeling, which disposes each member of the commu-
> nity to sever himself from the mass of his fellows, and to draw apart
> with his family and his friends; so that, after he has thus formed a little
> circle of his own, he willingly leaved society at large to itself.[3]

The "rugged individual" is the prototype of the American. *Individualism is a key American value, but* de Tocqueville saw it as potentially
dangerous. He wondered how a society could survive if its members
saw themselves as detached from the whole. De Tocqueville was right
to be concerned. Individualism is a counter-biblical value. The Bible
perceives people in right relationships, as a part of one body. When
we become Christians, we are intended for fellowship. We become
responsible for one another, and if necessary, to care for one another,
to admonish one another. Individualism questions both the right to do
that and the value of doing that. Society at large views each person
as a single unit that can make temporary allegiances without having to

bring values from other allegiances along. In business the idea that an employee or an employer should be accountable to an outside religious group is foreign to American ideals. While we are "on the job," we are expected to put aside our other relationships to the extent that they interfere with the organization's norms.

It is important to distinguish between individual*ism* and the idea that we are unique individuals who have been created in the image of God—a flawed image to be sure, but nevertheless, God's image. God sees us as individuals, loves us as individuals, walks with us as individuals. Individualism, on the other hand, allows us to place ourselves above God and over our fellows. Perhaps Paul's words in Romans 12:3 make the point: "Do not think of yourself more highly than you ought, but rather think of yourself with sober judgment in accordance with the measure of faith God has given you."

It is critical to note here that our individualism may be the major culprit in keeping us from experiencing ourselves as successful. Rather than finding our success in the success of our group or fellowship, to see ourselves as an integral part of the whole, we are encouraged to differentiate ourselves, to break away from the herd and compare ourselves with other individuals. How then can we become "successful" when there will always be *someone* who has done better than we have?

Materialism

The fourth American value we need to look at is *materialism*. The Puritans left a continent where people strongly believed in the concept of "limited good," the idea that there is only so much wealth in the world. If that is the case, then the only way one person can increase his wealth is at the expense of another. The pie is only so big, and if I got a bigger piece, you would get a smaller one. This concept did much to maintain class distinctions and to keep people in their place.

The settlers in this new land had come to a place of seemingly limitless natural resources. No "limited good" here! No scarcity of land, and apparently no limits to what an individual could own if he worked hard enough and had the good fortune of surviving. When one is placed in a country of seemingly limitless resources, freed from the restrictions of class and religion, and convinced of one's own individual rights, how natural it is to start acquiring things and to see those things as the measure of success. Today we honor such "successful" people. We believe (for the most part) that "anyone can make it in America." Material wealth in our minds gives us freedom to do and be what *we* want. The engine that drives all of this is "business." And business is what America has been about for most of our history. Consider this quote from Cotton Mather, a noted Puritan minister in 1695, only seventy-five years after the Pilgrims stepped ashore:

> Would a Man *Rise* by his Business? I say, then, let him *Rise* to his Business. It was foretold (Proverbs 22:29), Seest thou a man Diligent in his Business? *He shall stand before kings* . . . Yea, how can you ordinarily enjoy any rest at Night, if you have not been well at work in the Day? Let Business *engross* the most of your time.[4]

But as we have discovered, resources are not limitless. Nor does looking after business ensure the welfare of all. The Bible recognizes that there will be poor people in the world but refuses to accept this state of affairs. It asks that those of us who are not poor be concerned for the poor. With biblical justification the Roman Catholic conference "Vatican II" stated that God has a preference for the poor:

> He raises the poor from the dust and lifts the needy from the ash heap; he seats them with princes and has them inherit a throne of honor. For the foundations of the earth are the LORD's; upon them he has set the world. (1 Sam. 2:8)

> Do not go over your vineyard a second time or pick up the grapes that have fallen. Leave them for the poor and the alien. I am the LORD your God. (Lev. 19:10)

> If one of your countrymen becomes poor and is unable to support himself among you, help him as you would an alien or a temporary resident, so he can continue to live among you. (Lev. 25:35)

> "The Spirit of the Lord is on me, because he has anointed me to preach good news to the poor. He has sent me to proclaim freedom for the

prisoners and recovery of sight for the blind, to release the oppressed. (Luke 4:18)

Materialism works against the poor because it places more value on what *I* have than on what *we* have. It reduces people to objects. Not without cause do we speak of the god of Materialism.

"Business," particularly the publicly owned corporation, stands outside any family or social circle and operates independently. It becomes a mechanism to acquire material things. Its values lie in its own success. That is not to say that it is not controlled by the values of society, but rather that within those boundaries it pursues material success.

We can understand this more clearly if we compare a business with a not-for-profit organization such as the Red Cross, the Girl Scouts, or a Christian mission agency. Business has an ultimate goal—to stay in business. Its success is measured ultimately by its profitability to its owners or stockholders. It may have a number of social goals in terms of its conduct in its region, its concern for people, its concerns for its community. But if it does not produce a profit, it cannot stay in business. On the other hand, the not-for-profit organization has a variety of goals and a variety of "customers." Its ability to continue to operate is based on its proficiency in convincing its supporters that it is doing a worthwhile job, one in which they should invest their energy and money. The not-for-profit has no single "bottom line" but a variety of criteria with which to assess it performance.[5] By proclaiming itself as not-for-profit, it eschews the material values that naturally drive the business enterprise and seeks to supplant them with values that enhance society or a particular individual.

Competitiveness

The slogan "Anyone can make it in America" was the natural result of seemingly unlimited resources, equality, individualism, and materialism.

The consequence is that we Americans live in a particularly competitive society. Indeed, competitiveness is encouraged, both individually and corporately. Grades in school, win/lose records on the playing field, merit scholarships—all inculcate in us the idea that success has to do with doing better than someone else: "Winning isn't everything, it's the *only* thing." And most of us would agree that this is the natural order of things, especially in industrialized countries such as our own. But it's not the natural order; it doesn't have to be.

Some years ago a colleague of mine was transferred from New Zealand to Costa Rica, where he was the director of World Vision's Latin American region. I asked him how things were going with his children. "Oh, they are doing well. They are in the American school in San Jose."

"Any different from school in New Zealand?" I asked.

"The big difference is that they had to learn to *compete*. In New Zealand the kids were taught to work together. The American system pushes them to try to do better than their classmates."

Competitiveness pits one person against another. It puts high value on winning, on acquiring, on being "better" than someone else. Success is measured by comparing myself with how others are doing. It doesn't have to be so! We assume that competition is at the heart of business success. The Japanese have found a different solution. As companies they are fiercely competitive, but within the company there are other forces at work. It is understood that the good of the company (community) is more crucial than the good of the individual.

Capitalism

Few would disagree that *capitalism is a basic American value.* We examined it earlier. We mention it here only to recognize how it fits with other American values that we need to understand if we are to function as Christians in the workplace. The intent of capitalism is to produce a surplus that can be used to generate additional surplus. If we believe, as most Americans do, that there is unlimited wealth for all who would work for it, a "surplus" is potentially available to everyone. Unfortunately, no society has demonstrated that this ideal situation exists. The fact that we have over five million people in the United States who are not just poor, but desperately poor, is eloquent testimony that we have not yet found a way to care for those who, for whatever reason, have not been given opportunity to produce a surplus for themselves.

This is not to fault capitalism per se, but rather to remind us that as Christians we have a responsibility to understand capitalism's potential for marginalizing portions of any society and to try to find correctives. Capitalism believes in "free enterprise" and the wisdom of letting the marketplace decide losers and winners. The results can be disastrous for the losers who did not know they were even in the game.[6]

Each Generation Is Better Than the Last

A seventh American value that concerns us is part of what we might call "modernism." Briefly stated, *Americans believe that each generation knows more and is more intelligent than the previous one.* Up until now, each generation could claim that it was better educated than the last. Parents were convinced that their children were smarter and more capable than themselves.

This belief cuts us off from history. It leaves us with the conceit that as we have discovered new technological ideas, we have also uncovered new "truths" about human nature. I can remember when I first happened on the idea that the mark of a mature Christian was that he or she could confront the paradoxes of life and live peacefully with them. One had to recognize the seeming differences between such things as free will and God's sovereignty and just accept them both. I saw this as a new idea. I discovered it! Some years later I was reading F. Scott Fitzgerald and discovered he saw this ability as the mark of a gentleman. Then I read that Aristotle said the same thing! I was operating on the naive assumption that as a "modern man" I had discovered something new!

Solomon had it right. There is nothing new (about people) under the sun. But we keep believing that there is and that we have a handle on it. In recent years we have decried some manufacturers' goal of "planned obsolescence." Most of us think of this as a phenomenon peculiar to the twentieth century. But listen to this quote from de Toc-queville in 1831:

> I accost an American sailor, and inquire why the ships of his country are built so as to last for a short time; he answers without hesitation, that the art of navigation is every day making rapid progress, that the finest vessel would become almost useless if it lasted beyond a few years.[7]

Americans value the present over the past, and we do not have to look far to see this value at work in American Christianity. How many new churches have been founded on the belief that a new truth has been discovered, one that had supposedly remained hidden since biblical times?

There are many implications in this glorification of the present. If we as Christians attempt to apply (seemingly old) biblical values to business, we may be quickly labeled as old-fashioned, out of step with the times. Or we may just as easily conclude as Christians that the "old time religion" just won't work in this modern world. Not true. The Ten Commandments are just as valid today as they were thousands of years ago.

American Civil Religion

The last value to be examined is based on our understanding of America as a Christian nation. We are a religious people.

> The vast majority [of Americans] have orthodox Christian beliefs: they acknowledge the virgin birth, the death and resurrection of Jesus Christ, the power of prayer, the reality of the miracles of God, the importance of the Church, the reality of Satan and hell and the life of the Holy Spirit in Believers. More than nine out of ten adults own a Bible, and a majority of them believe it is God's written word, totally accurate in its teaching. Perhaps surprisingly, a majority of American adults— about three out of five—claim that they have made a personal commitment to Jesus Christ that is still important in their lives today.[8]

Why then, we might ask, don't we seem to *act* accordingly? That is the dilemma we Christians face. Some would say we just don't realize how "religious" we are. Gary Wills believes that much of this ignorance can be attributed to the American press. In his book *Under God* (1990), he sees the media as constantly surprised by the fact that a revival has broken out somewhere. After all, it was not too long ago that liberal theologians were pronouncing that God was dead. How is it that he keeps reappearing? Whether Wills's analysis is correct or not, it is a fact that *America has developed a civil religion*. This is not apparent today as it was ten to twenty years ago, but it still exists. Where did it come from? How does it operate as a value?[9]

The first settlers arrived with strong motivations to establish a new, basically religious society: the kingdom of God on earth. They came with well-set religious convictions about what that should be. In front of them lay what appeared to be unlimited opportunities. However, few, if any, of those original colonists thought about how radically their environment would change their attitudes about wealth, success, and their position in life. In a matter of two or three generations the dream of establishing the kingdom of God was forgotten by most. By the beginning of the eighteenth century, colonial America might have appeared to many to be a completely secularized society.

Just when it appeared that Christianity in America was a lost cause, the Holy Spirit intervened in such spectacular ways that the resulting phenomena became known as the Great Awakening. Beginning in New Jersey in 1720, religious revivals spread throughout the colonies. All over America people miraculously experienced a mighty overcoming of the Spirit. Evidences that God was in their midst were everywhere. Salvation was at hand. The kingdom of God was at hand. Could this be the long expected Millennium? Jonathan Edwards was not alone in believing so:

> It is not unlikely that this work of God's Spirit, so extraordinary and wonderful, is the dawning, or at least a prelude, of the glorious work of God, so often foretold in the Scriptures, which in the progress and issue of it, shall renew the work of mankind . . . We cannot reasonably think otherwise, than that at the beginning of this great work of

God must be near. That there are many things that make it probable that this work will begin in America.[10]

Carried out by mass revivals and itinerant evangelists, the Great Awakening set the tone for American evangelism for the next two hundred years. But at the same time the Enlightenment—the Age of Reason—was moving into high gear. The Great Awakening appealed to emotions and inner feelings, but the religion of the Enlightenment appealed to rational thought. "Reason" and "natural religion" became by-words of the day. Both ideas did much to shape today's civil religion.

Rationalism had two major religious aspects: the metaphysical oneness of the Deity (rationalism had no room for the doctrine of the Trinity); and the benevolent nature of God. God was good, and his goodness made unthinkable the doctrine of election: the idea that God would choose some for salvation and not choose others. The idea of God damning people was horrible. Original sin was repudiated. Humanity had within its power the ability to control its destiny. Although the Bible was divine revelation, each part had to be validated by reason.

Using human reason to test the Bible's validity is a continuing trend. A recent study by a group of so-called theologians decided that less than 80 percent of the words attributed to Jesus in the New Testament were actually spoken by him. The current debate over the church's attitude toward homosexual relationships reflects the same approach. The assumption is that "modern" people live in a world where biblical principles don't work.

Russell Rogers is a professor of business administration and a management consultant. In a speech in the spring of 1991 he made a telling observation about technological progress. He recounted how much he enjoyed futuristic space odysseys, such as "Star Wars" and "Star Trek," all demonstrating the inexorable progress of technology. Newer and more imaginative devices keep appearing. Transporters that convert people to molecules and then reassemble them elsewhere are the order of the day. In dramatic contrast is the second theme of these movies: *People don't change.* They are just as sinful, just as selfish, just as self-protective as they have always been. Evidently Hollywood sees very little hope for the advancement of humankind!

Returning to our brief history, it is significant that during the period when the Enlightenment *and* the Great Awakening were influencing the development of the church, the pressures of political control by England were becoming intolerable to the American colonists. They had become used to governing themselves through a legislative process that reflected the principle of the individual's "rights," and legislation without representation was abhorrent to them. But to keep the colonies as a source of raw material and at the same time prevent them from competing in areas of manufacturing, the British crown levied a series of taxes on them to control commerce. The colonies reacted strongly and declared their independence from Great Britain. When the British attempted to subdue them, the colonists were well prepared to deal with them. The Great Awakening had produced a new emphasis on education and new colleges and universities were founded. An extensive series of roads had been built; travel was easier. Weekly newspapers were common; communication was enhanced. All these factors combined to make it possible for the colonies to take concerted action against England. The result was the American Revolution.

The Declaration of Independence, around which the colonies rallied in 1776, and the Constitution, which established America's future course in 1789, are both pregnant with the language of the Enlightenment. It is easy for today's Christian to project evangelical Christianity back in history, but (as we noted earlier), when our Founding Fathers declared that it was "self-evident" that "all men are created equal," their argument was based on rationalism, not on the Bible. The men who gathered to write the Constitution were more children of the Enlightenment than they were ancestors of evangelical Christianity.

Benjamin Franklin stated the new nation's religious creed: "the existence of the Deity; that he made the world, and govern'd it by Providence; that the most acceptable service of God was the doing of good to men; that our souls are immortal; and that all crime will be punished, and virtue rewarded, either here or hereafter."[11] Franklin's ideas, promulgated by others, formed the three great fundamentals of America's religion: *the existence of God, the immortality of men,* and *man's accountability.* This Civil Religion[12] has survived the extremes of liberal and fundamentalist denominations. Notice that it does not speak of Christ. A Muslim could probably subscribe to it. Politicians regularly evoke this civil religion as they see the need. Their sensitivity is a testimony to the religiosity of America.

Reflections

Pluralism, equality, individualism, materialism, competitiveness, capitalism, the present over the past, and civil religion—all have an impact on our daily lives. The question that faces us is to what degree we should allow them to shape the personal values that ultimately determine how we will live and whether we will succeed and whether we will keep our faith.

Seven American values are listed below. After each one write a one-sentence statement on how this value affects your personal view of success, business, or faith.

1. Pluralism
2. Equality
3. Individualism
4. Materialism
5. Competitiveness
6. Capitalism
7. Civil religion

As you share your answers with others, what statements do you see that would reinforce your life as a Christian? Detract from it?

Unfortunately, most Americans see the organized church as ancillary to their individual Christianity. But the church is intended to be representative of a new society called the kingdom of God. The Pilgrims clearly understood that concept. The history of America explains how quickly the kingdom of God concept eroded; today the pluralism of America is reflected in the pluralism of Christian churches.

The Bible describes the church as the body of Christ and Christians as being parts of a body, intimately and dependently related to one another. American individualism tells us to go it alone. The Bible tells us that the Holy Spirit works through the church to help us find our directions, strength, and values. Without such a community we lose our most vital tool in finding success as Christians in business.

Today's Church

hy is it important for me to know about today's church in a discussion about Christians being successful in business?" If that is your question, this chapter is especially for you. The church is an integral part of success for the Christian in business. That sounds quite foreign to most American Christians. But to claim to be a Christian while not identifying with a local church is sub-biblical. The successful Christian is a committed Christian: committed to Christ and committed to a specific group of fellow believers, that the Bible calls a church. Unfortunately, most North Americans see the organized church as ancillary to their individual Christianity, and tend to think of "church" as merely a place or another group to join.

That certainly was my view as a teenager and young adult. My mother and father were Episcopalians. I was brought up in that denomination, was a regular attender at Sunday school, and a boy soprano in the Christmas pageant. At twelve I went through the process that hopefully confirmed the vows that my parents had made for me at infant baptism. I learned the Apostle's Creed, the Nicene Creed, and much of the Book of Common Prayer. But when I attended a Christian prep school, I was faced with a question: "Have you accepted Christ as your *personal* Savior?" This was a new idea for me. The emphasis here was not on the corporate experience but on the individual experience. Evangelical Christianity was concerned for individual salvation. Individual means of grace—prayer, Bible study, witnessing, Christ as "personal Savior"—has been the test of orthodoxy for evangelical Christians for the past hundred years. But what about a particular body of believers gathered in a local church? The Romans 12, 1 Corinthians 12, and Ephesians 4 passages were foreign to my understanding. I knew I was a Christian, but I didn't know what it meant to be a Christian in relationship to others. I had been introduced to the vital need to follow Christ, but no one told me I was needed in a special expression of the body of Christ called a local church.

The church is supposed to be representative of a new society called the kingdom of God. The church is *not* the kingdom of God, but it is the evidence that the kingdom of God has broken in on humanity. With all of its flaws and diversity, the church in its many different expressions around the world gives witness to the truth and the reality of Father, Son, and Holy Spirit and the eternal values that undergird the kingdom. Through the centuries the church has been the shaper of values, the carrier and teacher of the Christian understanding of what the world is all about. The Holy Spirit has worked through the church to forge the Judeo-Christian heritage which is the foundation of our society, our laws, and our attitudes. The church has more potential for changing the society for good than any other institution in the United States.

However, the church does not exist only in its local expression, its local parish; it is also expressed in a myriad of organizations, coalitions, and institutions. But the home base for every Christian is a local church, and without that base we fight a lonely and frustrating battle to be biblical Christians in an increasingly counter-biblical world.

North American Church History

It was helpful for us to understand the history of business in North America. Similarly it is helpful to trace the history of the church in North America,[1] to see how our particular expression of Christianity has been shaped—positively and negatively.

Christians with other opinions were arriving elsewhere. In 1607 English adventurers had settled in the Chesapeake Bay area and founded Jamestown. Through a series of misadventures the company charter was returned to the English crown in 1622, and the subsequent settlers were predominantly Anglicans. The first Quakers appeared in Boston in 1656. The first Baptist association was formed in 1670. In 1681 William Penn and his Quaker constituents were given a charter to found a new colony in Pennsylvania.

By the end of the seventeenth century religious ardor had cooled in the colonies but the church was renewed and refurbished by the Great Awakening, beginning with pastors of four Dutch Reformed churches in New Jersey. Revival spread across the colonies. With the arrival of George Whitefield in 1740, revival filled the Atlantic seaboard:

> The Great Awakening drew many results in its wake. It brought numerous converts into the churches, though the exact number cannot be determined, and made Christianity more a religion of the people than it had ever been before in the American colonies. It quickened the spiritual interest of great numbers of those already in the churches. Along with the Enlightenment, it stimulated humanitarian and philanthropic interests of which the eloquent and promotionally gifted Whitefield was a notable example. . . . [The] revival ignored many of the old alignments based on theology and church government, and created new alignments by *making personal conversion the supreme test question. Thus the way was prepared for the pragmatic ignoring of theoretical questions in favor of direct experience and practical results that became so popular in America.*
>
> The Awakening also hastened the separation of church and state. It emphasized the individual Christian and his inner religious experience than the church or theocracy [italics mine].[2]

> The social effects of the Great Awakening cannot be ignored. The Awakening elevated the common man. By giving him self-authenticating religious experience it made him independent of professional ministers and church synods.[3]

Churches of many different doctrinal persuasions were affected. This multiplicity of religious views within one country was a new phenomenon in the world. Prior to this time every nation-state had its state religion. Many wondered if it was possible to create a nation-state with such a plurality of belief. Thus, when the time came for the thirteen colonies to declare their independence and create the United States of America, Thomas Jefferson wondered out loud whether this "lively experiment" could succeed.[4] But the experiment *did* succeed.

The vast majority of the Christians in the new country were Protestants. (Those who were not Christians were mostly Deists.) Thus, they were able to describe themselves as "One nation under God" and to put "In God We Trust" on their money and still maintain a constitutional "separation" of church and state. The Sabbath was widely respected throughout the nation. British common law was augmented by formalized laws, all of which assumed a common religious heritage. The Ten Commandments were held up by every denomination as foundational to being a Christian. America may not have been Lutheran or Presbyterian or Roman Catholic, but everyone understood that it was a Christian nation.

Manifest Destiny

The idea that the United States had a "manifest destiny" under God was almost universally accepted through the nineteenth century. The expansive optimism that was bred into the American character led many to believe that what was happening in the United States was nothing less than the millennial reign of Christ described in Revelation 20. This view gained momentum as the nation put itself back together after a bloody Civil War. It led to an attempt to balance what one believed with what one did. If this was the millennium, then we needed to practice our Christianity.

Even though the nation was rapidly industrializing, until the twentieth century most people continued to think of everyday life as a whole. They didn't see themselves pulled apart by the competing roles they had to play. The majority lived, grew up, and died in the same town or city in which they were born. They followed the denominational preference of their parents and were impacted very little by information from the outside world. Things *were* getting better, and the dominant view was that they would continue to get better.

A Different View of the Millennium

But many Christians were rethinking this optimistic view. Early twentieth-century euphoria was soon shattered by the First World War. There were serious divisions within denominations, primarily among the Presbyterians and the Baptists.[5] Until 1860 most Christians were "postmillennialists." That is, they thought that the glorious millennium spoken of in the Bible had already occurred, and they were a part of it. Many Christians quickly swung from this postmillennial view that they were on a track to heaven, to a premillennial view which saw the world heading for disaster. This shift also caused many people to rethink what it meant to be a Christian, and to reexamine the mission of the church. If Christ was going to return in the clouds to claim his own before the millennium, and if the world was approaching Armageddon, then the primary task of the church was to warn the world of pending doom. The church must call sinners to repentance, save as many people as possible, and snatch them from the flames of hell. Social concerns were secondary, for what good did it do to improve life here if life in the hereafter was eternal separation from God?

But what about the rest of the mission of the church? What about caring for the poor and the widows, visiting those in prison? What about the need for social reform? There were a large number of Christians who thought that these objectives had equal or more importance. The debate led to the evolution of what today we call Fundamentalism, a title reinforced by the definitive doctrinal writings of J. Gresham Machen titled *The Fundamentals*, which George Marsden describes so well.[6] By 1924 the lines were completely drawn, and Fundamentalists claimed to be the only true Christians in the United States. On the opposite side were those who believed in a "social gospel." They branded the Fundamentalists' insistence on the primacy of Scripture as Neanderthal and the Fundamentalists as anti-intellectuals. These "liberals" saw the gospel as much more amenable to the rationalism produced by the Enlightenment and the new theory of evolution. The Fundamentalists' attempt to keep such teaching out of the public schools reached its height in a classic battle between William Jennings Bryan and Clarence Darrow at the so-called Scopes "Monkey Trial" in 1925.

The Great Depression of the 1930s seemed to bear out the Fundamentalists' premillennial view. Things were certainly getting worse, not better. America's entry into World War II in December 1941 encouraged that belief.

But other forces were at work. While the Fundamentalist debate waxed hottest within Baptist and Presbyterian groups, renewal was coming from other quarters. The first part of this century saw the rapid growth of Pentecostal denominations such as the Assemblies of God and the Four Square Churches. Here the emphasis on experiencing the manifestations of the Holy Spirit harked back to the days of the Great Awakening with its numerous outward evidences of inward experience. It is a helpful oversimplification to say that the ideology of the Protestant Church of the early twentieth century was divided into the Fundamentalists' emphasis on what one *believed*, the "mainline" denominations' emphasis on what one *did,* and the Pentecostal emphasis on what one *experienced*. All three emphases are with us today.

Fundamentalists saw the postwar era as a special opportunity from God to evangelize the world. Thousands of men and women trained in nondenominational Bible schools and colleges were sent as foreign missionaries by independent "faith" missions. While this flood of Fundamentalist missionaries rose, mainline denominations in the United States were curtailing their cross-cultural missionary efforts. It was reasoned that since churches had been started in most countries of the world, the task of the American churches was to cooperate with these churches, recognize their autonomy, and learn from them. Mission was seen "from six continents to six continents."

The Neo-Evangelicals

Immediately following World War II, Christian theologians within the Fundamentalist ranks saw the need for academic integrity and theological expertise. Labeled as Neo-Evangelicals, these men founded Fuller Theological Seminary in Pasadena, California, in the 1940s and set out to gain mainline acceptance and understanding of those of evangelical persuasions. The writings of Edward John Carnell, Carl F. H. Henry, Wilbur Smith, Gleason Archer, George Ladd, and Everett Harrison, focused scholarly attention on many theological and sociological issues that faced the church. Carl Henry's *The Uneasy Conscience of Modern Fundamentalism* called Fundamentalists to a more balanced view of life and mission and his *Remaking of the Modern Mind* sought to bring thoughtful scholarship back to Fundamentalist theology. Carnell's *The Case for Orthodox Theology* and *Christian Commitment* described a fuller, rounded Christianity. George Ladd's *Jesus and the Kingdom* opened up a renewed understanding of the meaning of the kingdom of God.

During this same period the mainline denominations were trying to chart new directions of unity under the influence of the World Council of Churches and the National Council of Churches. Some denominations were exploring the possibility of merging as part of the Ecumenical Movement. However, the National Council and denominational leaders consistently moved too far ahead of their lay constituency. Almost every denomination faced internal challenges from their evangelical members and individual churches. Spiritual renewal movements proliferated. Separate efforts at more evangelical mission enterprises were demanded by the laity in many denominations.

At the same time a different kind of renewal was moving through all the denominations in the form of the Charismatic Movement. With its emphasis on the power of the Holy Spirit to change the physical and social dynamics of individual lives, the Charismatic Movement found a ready acceptance among clergy and laity who were searching for a meaningful *experience* of what it meant to be a Christian.

The Church and Culture

In this brief history we can see the impact of American culture on the church. The pluralism of the early settlers and the vastness of the country provided a fertile seedbed for new doctrines and new ways of living. American individualism encouraged an individualistic, personal religion. The rejection of seemingly abstract theological concepts was fostered by both individualism and the disappearance from most mainline denominations of any profound inner experience that would give authenticity to the joy that was supposed to accompany the Christian life. The increasing pressures of a secularized and technological society intensified the search for life's meaning which mainline denominations seemed unable to fulfill.

While mainline churches were fighting a losing battle against change, evangelical churches were going through their own metamorphosis. The burst of academic energy that had begun with the founding of Fuller Theological Seminary was followed by an increasing sophistication on the part of evangelical lay persons. Their new understanding of the gospel's message was that it not only called men and women away from sin but also called them to be active servants of Christ in a needy world.

Today's Churches

Isolation

The majority of local churches have become retreat centers for their members. Here we find people like us, people who mostly understand what it means to be a Christian. Here we find a set of values, customs, and rules that defines how we act out our role as Christians while we are together. These roles are supported by a specialized language whose phrases and ideas are seldom heard in the workplace. The result is that we lack thought forms and means of expression to communicate what we believe to those who don't believe.[7] There is nothing wrong with Christian jargon. Like all jargon it allows us to communicate more effectively to our own in-group. Most of our roles have a set of special ideas and words. What is missing is "bridging ideas" that mean the same thing in different situations, and therefore are understandable to people in other groups who are playing other roles.

Pluralism

From the Pilgrims' idea of a city of God within which there would be a common understanding and a common life worked out in light of God's Word, churches in the United States have evolved into a multiplicity of denominations and an immense mosaic of individual churches. The pluralism of America is reflected in the pluralism of its churches. Religion and society have interacted to form and shape each other. This pluralism has both negatives and positives. In many ways it reflects the healthy pluralism of the early church before it became a state church under the Emperor Constantine in A.D. 313. The legality of different customs in different churches was affirmed by the Council of Jerusalem (Acts 15), and the spread of a house-church movement throughout the Roman Empire was based on a common belief in a resurrected Jesus rather than in any intention to form a particular type of church government. Christianity itself sees individuals as specially and separately gifted for the purpose of fitting together to be a local church.

The negative side is the division caused by our natural tendency to believe that our own particularly held beliefs are *right*, and thus the contrary beliefs of others are *wrong*. It is very difficult to hold a belief strongly while at the same time allowing others to hold a differing view. We need to go back again to the counsel of Paul:

> One man considers one day more sacred than another; another man considers every day alike. Each one should be fully convinced in his own mind. He who regards one day as special, does so to the Lord. He who eats meat, eats to the Lord, for he gives thanks to God; and he who abstains, does so to the Lord and gives thanks to God (Rom. 14:5–6).

Designer Churches

The result of all of this diversity has been the growth and proliferation during the last fifteen years of what have been called "designer" churches. Why designer churches? Because local groups of Christians are inventing and reinventing new expressions of the church that meet their particular needs and reflect their understanding of what it means to be a church and to be Christians within that church.

What are some needs that lead to the formation of a designer church?

1. There is a need to find the kind of support that was once found in the extended family, where children, parents, singles, and widowed and divorced persons can find "family."
2. There is a need to find others who share similar difficulties, places where multiple self-help groups can help the individual not only manage life better, but also find reassurance in the fact that others are facing the same problems.
3. There is a need to find a sense of community based on some commonly shared values as a counterbalance to the do-it-yourself approach of the "me" generation of the 1980s.
4. There is a need to find an outlet for social service, to believe that one has contributed to the welfare of society based on strongly held convictions.
5. There is a need to see the gospel in action in the community.

I suspect that many of those are *your* needs. They are more than felt needs that arise out of life in general. Finding success is an almost impossible uphill battle unless you are part of an affirming, accepting community which will not only help define "success," but also will offer encouragement to be the kind of person you must become to be successful in your eyes and God's eyes.

The Church's Attitude Toward Business

What does the church think about business? *Not much.* "Good businessmen" are seen as needed to manage the Board of Trustees, but there is general agreement that a church can't be run like a business. That is only a partial truth. From years of interacting with pastors and lay people, I know that managing a church is much more difficult than running a business, but a church should be run *at least* as well as a business! Few are.

The bottom line for a business is an honest profit made in a socially acceptable manner. The bottom line for a church is much more diffuse. The church needs to see itself as somewhat like a vertically integrated business, such as Ford Motor Car Company used to be. At one time Ford prided itself in owning and controlling all the production processes from mining coal and iron to distributing the product. A church is like that. No part of human life is potentially outside its notice or concern. It calls people to repentance and faith. It nurtures its members to spiritual and social responsibility. It is in the business of "building" itself up in love (Eph. 4:16) and then sacrificing itself for the world. But in its attempt to keep itself unspotted from a polluting world, it often becomes other-worldly. Too often business has been equated with worldliness.

When we consider how business has often abused and debased people, we understand how the church developed such an attitude. But a deeper reflection is needed. The world is God's creation. It operates according to his rules. We see those rules reflected in his Word. We also stumble on them quite apart from his Word. People are continually learning new things about how the world works. It is ridiculous to ignore new understandings because the discoverers are not Christians, or even anti-Christians. But that reaction is far too common.

The result is that the church has usually lagged behind "the world" in adopting new and better ways to live and work together. A review of current management literature quickly reinforces the point. We read of the ultimate importance of people, of the need for teams, of group participation. The president of General Motors' new Saturn division tells us that what makes good cars is good people. Business has been forced to learn what makes people tick, how to manage in ways that most pastors would approve, if they knew more about it. Few churches appreciate their business people as a window on the world and fewer still provide business people with opportunities to discuss in depth the integration of business and Christian values.

Reflections

The church of which you and I are a part has a set of core beliefs, but as the number of sub-cultures grows, both ethnic and social, the addition of a multitude of other beliefs and programs will produce more and more designer churches. This in turn will make it increasingly difficult for individual Christians, especially Christian business people, to find "people like us." The result is that our ability to define Christian ethics, morals, and manners will become more and more difficult.

So it is imperative that we join others in a search for a biblical community. The church is intended by God to be our core family. It is the community to which we are to hold our allegiance and from which we are to derive our strength and fellowship. We have no alternative except to search for appropriate values together, trusting for guidance from the Holy Spirit.

1. Are you a member of a local church? If not, why not? If not, how do you get support from fellow Christians?

2. What are the positive features of your local church, those things that help you sort through the meaning of life in general and life in the workplace?

3. Look at the list on page 122. Are any of them your needs? What other needs do you have that are not being met by the church?

4. Based on your reading and your reflections thus far, do you think you can find success on your own? If not, how could the church be helping?

Faith maturity" is a measure of how we have integrated what we believe with how we act. Those who are mature in faith know that what we do is a reflection of what we believe or don't believe.

American evangelicals believe that it is only through God's grace and through faith that we become children of God. But a maturing faith moves beyond a propositional understanding of Christianity to one that sees Christians as citizens of the kingdom of God.

A faith that acts will stay strong in the face of ethical challenges we meet each day.

7

Today's Christian

I don't know what kind of a Christian you are. Perhaps you are not a Christian. But the chances are that if you have purchased this book, you believe you have a faith that you don't want to lose.

What is a Christian? What does it mean to *be* a Christian? It would be nice if there were one simple answer. On the one hand, it is as simple as saying, "I love Jesus." On the other hand, it is as difficult as saying, "Yes, but what are the implications of believing in Jesus? How does one act? What does one do? How can I tell who is or who is not a Christian?" The Bible is clear that it is not anything you or I have done or will do that makes us children of God. God's mercy—God's choice—God's love—God's grace. Those are the factors that make one a Christian. If that is true, there can be all kinds of Christians.

Let's try to narrow our discussion down some. We need to understand what American Christians think about themselves before we can talk intelligently about living out our Christian life in the United States.

What All Christians Believe

At the risk that all generalizations bring to anything, we can start by saying that by definition all Christians believe in Christ. More specifically, they believe that Jesus Christ is the Son of God and that he lived, died, and was brought back to life by the power of God. Thus he demonstrated his claim to be the Son of God. All Christians accept the Bible as their basic reference book. All evangelical Christians accept the Bible as the inspired, infallible Word of God within which one may not only find the basis of salvation but may also discover what it means to live out a Christian life. More "liberal" Christians may disagree with both the infallibility and the direct inspiration of Scripture, but they would be quick to say that it is from the Bible that we get our understanding of Christianity, and without the Bible today's Christianity would not exist. The Bible doesn't really have to prove itself. No other book in history has had such a profound effect on man, woman, social structures, ethics, morals, and ideas.

Faith Maturity

Let's take our discussion a step further. In the marvelous pluralism of the United States, there is huge diversity within the spectrum of Christianity that is anchored at one end by fundamentalism and at the other end by liberalism. There are a multitude of Protestant denominations in the United States. There are 350,000 churches within these denominations. In addition, there are 50,000 so-called independent or nondenominational churches. We can classify these various denominations by their tradition, such as Anglican, Reformed, Holiness, Pentecostal. Within each one of these groups we can also find further differentiation. But for our purposes a more helpful distinction might be to differentiate between Christians who put a strong emphasis on what they *believe* and those who put as strong an emphasis on what they *do*. Another way of saying this, which is not quite the same, would be to distinguish between those Christians who are more concerned about their relationship with God (vertical) from those who are more concerned about their relationship with others (horizontal).

In 1989 the Search Institute of Minneapolis received a grant from the Lily Foundation to measure the "faith maturity" of mainline denominations. The research was done within the context of wanting to know why membership in mainline denominations was declining and what could be done to reverse this condition. The phrase *faith maturity* was used to describe a person who had found a wholeness to life, a balance between the vertical and the horizontal dimensions. Of the 361 churches that were studied, the researchers found 52 churches with a high incidence of faith maturity. The people in these congregations had a strong faith and were working out their faith in a joyful and productive way.

The Search Institute's quest was the right one, and it is the right one for us as we attempt to describe today's Christian in the United States. The study showed that congregations with strong faith maturity were peopled by individuals and families who were involved with one another and with the world. A broad balance of programs was available. There were opportunities for its members to relate to, work with, study with, and debate with other people. The researchers drew the conclusion that congregations with strong faith maturity need a broad spectrum of programs. However, there is another possible explanation, one which needs to be explored much further. The opposite may be true: congregations that have strong faith maturity are congregations which *produce* such opportunities. It was the already existing faith maturity that recognized the need for horizontal relationships in response to a strong vertical relationship. The question then remains, "From whence came the faith maturity?" I would contend that faith maturity comes first from a strong belief.

The Importance of Belief

Since belief is fundamental to Christianity, Christians through the years have tried to enunciate what it is they believe. Paul's quotation in Philippians 2:6–11 is probably an early Christian hymn which was a statement of belief. The Apostle's Creed, shaped in its final form sometime before A.D. 390, was one of the early attempts to come up with a simple statement of faith. The Nicene Creed which was produced by the Council of Nicea in A.D. 325 was primarily the result of the church's wrestling with what did it mean when they said "Jesus is God." Through the years the church has sought to explain its belief to herself and to the world.[1] Notice the strong, evangelical affirmations of the Apostle's Creed:

> I believe in God the Father Almighty, Maker of heaven and earth, and in Jesus Christ his only Son our Lord, who was conceived by the Holy Ghost, born of the Virgin Mary, suffered under Pontius Pilate, was crucified, dead, and buried. He descended into hell; the third day he rose again from the dead. He ascended into heaven, and sitteth on the right hand of God the Father Almighty. From thence he shall come to judge the quick (living) and the dead.
> I believe in the Holy Spirit, the holy catholic (universal) church, the communion of saints, the forgiveness of sins, the resurrection of the body, and the life everlasting.

The Fundamentalist controversy (described briefly in chapter 6) resulted in a renewed strong statement of beliefs, *The Fundamentals*. As new Christian organizations were founded after World War II, it became important that each have a statement of faith. Thus, when World Vision was founded in 1950, it was thought important to utilize the statement of faith of the National Association of Evangelicals. When World Vision reorganized itself into an international organization in 1978, it was felt critical to maintain this statement of faith:

1. We believe that there is one God, eternally existent in three persons Father, Son and Holy Spirit.
2. We believe in the deity of our Lord Jesus Christ, in His virgin birth, in His sinless life, in His miracles, in His vicarious and atoning death through His shed blood, in His bodily resurrection, in His ascension to the right hand of the Father, and His personal return in power and glory.

3. We believe the Bible to be the inspired, the only infallible, authoritative Word of God.
4. We believe that for the salvation of lost and sinful man regeneration by the Holy Spirit is absolutely essential.
5. We believe in the present ministry of the Holy Spirit by whose indwelling the Christian is enabled to live a godly life.
6. We believe in the resurrection of both the saved and the lost. They that are saved unto resurrection of life and they that are lost unto the resurrection of damnation.
7. We believe in the spiritual unity of believers in our Lord Jesus Christ.

However, as World Vision carries out its joint ministries of mercy and evangelism in the world, it is continually faced with the question, "Yes, but what do you do?" Statements of faith are a good beginning place. What is important are the implications of that faith. James, in his short letter to the churches, says, "Show me your faith without deeds, and I will show you my faith by what I do" (James 2:18).

In other words, it is a question of propositional Christianity over and against performance theology. It is of ultimate concern what you believe. This belief was given to you by faith, as a free gift. But the biblical question is, "Does your life measure up to your beliefs?" We say we believe in gravity. We demonstrate that by not walking off hundred-foot cliffs or trying to roll balls uphill. We say we believe in the power of electricity. This causes us to act carefully when handling live wires and to expect all kinds of results when we switch on an electrical appliance. Americans have a marvelous ability to differentiate between what they believe and what they do. We are used to holding a wide range of ideas that have no implications for us.

Some years ago one of the humorous stories going around was about the man who claimed that in his family he made all the big decisions. When asked what decisions his wife made he replied, "Oh, she makes decisions on what kind of car we should buy or where we should live."

"Well, what decisions do you make?"

"I make the important ones, for example, should we let China join the United Nations."

Big talk. No action.

Mahatma Gandhi's counsel to Christians who wanted to evangelize Hindus was that if Christians started acting like Jesus, Hindus would respond to Christ by the hundreds of thousands.

Privatized Religion

The bottom line of this big-talk-no-action syndrome is that most American Christians privatize their religion. We are grateful for it and rejoice with one another about it. We may even believe that people who do not know Christ are eternally damned. But since we have not seen many positive results from sharing our faith, we tend to place this apparent ineffectiveness in the same category with the problems that we see in behaving Christianly in our business.

Even though the average American Christian's behavior in the business world may not demonstrate a high correlation between belief and action, in the *Christian* world this is not true. Christians tend to play the roles that we talked about in chapter 5 very well. We have a standard vocabulary that we use within our particular group. We have code words which identify us. If I tell you about my experience in "coming to a personal relationship with Jesus Christ," you can immediately place me in relationship to your understanding of Christianity. We have this marvelous ability to tailor our responses to fit our surroundings. When hearing from some Christians we are entertaining in our home that they have been greatly blessed, we may aptly respond, "Praise the Lord!" When told by our fellow-workers that the company has just gotten a new major contract, we reply, "Hey, that's great!" (On the other hand, "hell" and "damn" may be our normal responses to a bad situation in the office, but eyebrows would certainly be raised if that was our response to a difficulty in the church.)

Privatized religion is also evidenced in the generational differences among Christians in the United States. Although the majority say they read the Bible at least once a month, the kinds of Bible study and expository preaching that were part of the everyday experience of my generation of Christians is not normative for Baby Boomers nor Baby Busters. Only a minority of Christians in the United States would be as conversant with the Bible as they were with their physics text in high school or college. Statements of faith have also gone out of style. The good side of that is that "faith without works is dead." The bad side of all this is when the average Christian is asked for a systematic explanation of what he or she believes are Christianity's foundational truths, he or she has to start from scratch.

Since most churches in the United States do not seem to have a fundamental understanding of what it means to be the body of Christ, few American Christians understand this. Individualism leads us to expect that we should be able to make decisions alone, or certainly within the confines of our family. The idea that we are organically linked to another group of people who may also have some insight as to the leading of the Spirit in our lives is outside our comprehension.

This same phenomenon is at work in our business life where we tend to keep our religious beliefs to ourselves. Consequently, we may be working with Christians all around us, but we never know that. (After all, if 42 percent of the population is in church on Sunday, there is a good chance that 42 percent of our fellow-workers were in church last Sunday!) Even when we do identify fellow Christians, we are much more likely to talk about our religious experience than to discuss what Christianity has to do with how we behave at work. Many of us would think it was very "unbusinesslike" to get together with other employees to discuss our company's ethics.

Religion as a Role

Is your Christianity another role you play? Does the language you use and the thought forms you work with depend on whether you are with other Christians or at church? That's the way it is for many of us. Think of three different situations with the same problem: settings at work, at home, and at church. Let's discuss a problem—repairing water damage—in one case your office, in the next case your living room, and in the last case, your church Sunday school building.

Scene One
We are talking to the head of maintenance.
"Joe, this is a mess. How did it happen?"
Joe responds, "Well, Bill, one of the maintenance men left the water running in the janitor's closet over the weekend. This is the third time he has done something like this. Says he's sorry, Bill."
"Sorry! This is going to cost us over $1,000! Joe, he's out the door."

Scene Two
You are talking to your son.
"Billy, this is a mess. How did it happen?"
Billy responds, "Dad, I left the water running in the upstairs sink, and it overflowed and came down through the ceiling. I can't imagine how I did that. I'm sorry, Dad."
"Billy, you're going to be a lot sorrier. This is going to come out of your allowance and your money from your paper route."

Scene Three
You are talking to a fellow deacon at church.
"Bob, this is a mess. How did it happen?"
Bob responds, "Bill, as far as we can tell someone left the water running in the janitor's closet. I can't imagine who would do a thing like that. Some kids, do you think?"
"Bob, I hope not. We need to really be in prayer about our young people. It's a tough world out there."

In the first scene there was no thought for the maintenance man about to be discharged. In the second case, family values intervened. In the last case, you saw the situation through eyes of grace and the need of the perpetrator. What you see is that you have been applying different values to different situations. The struggle you face to make your Christianity real is to learn to *think* christianly, to apply the same set of values to each situation.

First, however, you have to understand your own values and the values of your fellow Christians, which you may assume are the same as yours, but may be quite surprised to learn otherwise when you really dig into another person's head. This is not something you can do as an individual. Your individualism, in fact, keeps you from doing it. What you need are other men and women who can set out on the journey with you.

A great deal has been learned by using the "case-study method" to try to understand our reactions in different situations. The case-study method was used at the Harvard Business School to expose future MBAs to the problems they would face later. The approach is to tell the story up to the point where a decision needs to be made. The group, having heard the story to this point, then discusses what they believe would be the appropriate solution to the dilemma and why. There is not necessarily a "right" answer to the problem. Rather the approach is to help one another see solutions to business dilemmas. In their book *Full Value: Cases in Christian Business Ethics* (1978), Oliver Williams and John Houck present a series of cases from both small and large companies. One of the cases tells the story of John Karen who had been trained as an engineer and through a series of circumstances had moved into the textile business. After discussing his struggles as a Christian executive in a highly competitive business, Karen goes on to say:

> "A question I'm frequently asked is: 'Can a person be both a business executive and a Christian at the same time?'
>
> "First, I'd like to change the question to 'Can you *try* to be a business executive; can you try to be a true Christian?' There are immense difficulties in being either one of them, let alone mixing them together. Yet, I believe it can be done.
>
> "I reject the argument that one cannot be a Christian and be a successful business person. Likewise, I reject the argument that Christianity somehow ratifies what an executive does. I see myself living out a synthesis of two powerful worlds. Sometimes I am pulled toward one, and the other times I am pulled toward the other.
>
> "Now to get out of this bind, the first thing is for the Christian business person to be constantly seeking and asking: 'Is there a Christian value or ethical aspect of the problem we're considering? Have we missed anything because we are so wrapped up in approximate, obvious dimensions of the operations?'"[2]

These kinds of case studies can be very helpful. The bottom line is that you can't go it alone. You need the help of other Christian businessmen and women.

Reflections

1. Are there other Christians in your company? How many of them do you know personally?

2. To what extent have you discussed with other Christians the dilemmas of matching your faith with your performance on the job, as well as the company's performance?

3. What do you think would happen if you brought together a group of Christians within your company to discuss "Christian values"? What resources would you need? How would you go about discussing what Christian values are?

The world has become so accustomed to expecting the worst that it is almost impossible to expect the best. The kingdom of God that was announced by Jesus makes no sense to people who want to sit on top of the mountain and own all they survey.

Matthew's Gospel tells us that Jesus came to announce the good news that God's kingdom had broken into history. This is an upside down kingdom where the poor are lifted up, where people act in the interest of others, where the qualities of a small child are held up as those needed to enter the kingdom.

Becoming active citizens of the kingdom of God is a matter of opening our minds to what God would teach us. As we do that, we will redefine for ourselves the meaning of "success."

Life in God's Kingdom

"Now Cain said to his brother Abel, 'Let's go out to the field.' And while they were in the field, Cain attacked his brother Abel and killed him. . . . Cain said to the Lord, 'My punishment is more than I can bear. Today you are driving me from the land and I will be hidden from your presence; I will be a restless wanderer on the earth, and whoever finds me will kill me'" (Gen. 4:8, 13–14).

A restless wanderer on the earth. Cut off from the presence of God. Lonely. Isolated. Alienated. No longer knowing and being known. The human story is one of people rising up against one another, crusting over their lives by seeking their own good at the expense of others. Sin has to do with the breaking of relationships. Justice, goodness, mercy, kindness, truthfulness are all relationship terms. We sin by not doing right to others, either by withholding what is right or actively doing wrong.

To protect itself, each society develops laws. Some of these laws are civil laws, designed to work for a more efficient society. Others are criminal laws, designed to protect us physically from one another.

In addition, societies need protection from other societies. Alienation between nations is as common as alienation between people. And so we attempt to construct international forums, such as the United Nations and the European Economic Community, to somehow protect us from one another.

Good News and Bad News

God breaks into this world of alienation with his continuing covenant of love. He calls out a people for himself, a people to demonstrate by their life together how God intended for us to live. He announces that we shall have no other gods before him. He instructs us how we should live together. He defines the meaning of justice for us. He models for us what it means to love. The human story is an ongoing saga of God loving people to himself and thus loving them toward one another. And when words were not enough, when God's acts of justice were not enough, he modeled for us what it means to make the ultimate sacrifice. "And being found in appearance as a man, he humbled himself and became obedient to death—even death on a cross!" (Phil. 2:8).

The bad news of history has been our hopeless loneliness. The good news is that the Maker of the Universe loves us and calls us to be with him through eternity.

The world has become so accustomed to expecting the worst that it is almost incomprehensible to expect the best. The kingdom of God that was announced by Jesus makes no sense to people who want to sit at the top of the mountain and own all they survey. Why should people think of others first? Is not the rugged individualism that has been the hallmark of our country the model to be admired? Can there be any profit in turning the cheek, in walking the extra mile?

Yes! No matter how foreign that may be to our day-to-day experience. Yes!

Our rational minds demand a demonstration. Where can we find one? The biblical answer is summed up in two verses in the Gospel of John: "By this all men will know you are my disciples, if you love one another" (13:35). And Jesus praying, "I in them and you in me. May they be brought into complete unity to let the world know that you sent me and have loved them even as you have loved me" (17:23).

A Community of Believers

The Bible tells us that we are designed and individually gifted for community:

> It was he who gave some to be apostles, some to be prophets, some to be evangelists, and some to be pastors and teachers, to prepare God's people for works of service, so that the body of Christ may be built up until we all reach unity in the faith and in the knowledge of the son of God and become mature, attaining to the whole measure of the full-ness of Christ (Eph. 4:11–13).

When you became a Christian, a you-shaped space opened up in a local body of believers. You were needed there right then. You didn't have to be trained to be part of this body, any more than you had to become a good person before you were acceptable to God and a candidate for his forgiveness. You were called out of your individualism back to relationships.

Let me make a very important aside here. In recent years we have seen the development of evangelistic methods that call people to confession and forgiveness without ever explaining to them that the result of these actions is not only a new relationship with God, but also a new relationship with the people of God. The ultimate example of this is the televangelist who is satisfied to leave people connected to the body of Christ only by their television set. In other words, no connection.[1] My sisters, my brothers! The Bible knows of no such kind of Christians. Jesus announced the kingdom and new life in that kingdom. He called people to repentance so that they might share this life. He calls people to himself, but he does that through the medium of his body, the church. The church is not a social or moral body per se. It's a mystical body. *To not be connected to a local church is sub-Christian.*

I can immediately hear the thoughts going through your mind. Perhaps you are saying with many others, "If the local church that *I* know is supposed to be an example of God's love, that's not very good evidence." Of course, you are right. In sharing an early outline of this book with my good friend David Fraser, he commented, "Perhaps a better title would be *How to Succeed in the Church without Losing Your Faith!*" The kingdom is coming, but it has not completely arrived. The very fact that I am struggling with you on these pages to discover how to live the life that is Christian is a mute testimony to that fact.

When we become Christians we have an immediate desire to ask with Paul, "Lord, what would you have me to do?" What the Lord would have us to do is to first be in right relationship to our sisters and brothers. Let's think about that.

Some years ago I was asked, "Do you pray over all your decisions?" It sounded like a very spiritual question, and I was ashamed to admit that I didn't consciously pray over all my decisions. But it certainly got me to wondering whether I should—and if I should, why I didn't. I finally came to what I believed was God's intention for me. The next time someone asked me that question, I thought I would have an answer. Finally that day came. (Perhaps I did a little prompting!)

"Do you pray over all your decisions?"

"No, I don't."

"What *do* you do?"

"I check my love life."

"You *what*?!"

"I check my love life. I first heard St. Augustine's famous statement 'Love God and do as you please' in seminary. I've been pondering on that. I can see what St. Augustine meant. If I love the Lord God with all my heart and soul and mind, there is a good possibility that what *I* please will be pleasing to him. But then I got to wondering about how I would know I was pleasing God. I thought about Jesus' statement to his disciples, 'Men will know you are my disciples in that you love one another. A new commandment I give you that you love one another' (John 13:35). I figure that if I am really loving my neighbor as myself, I'm probably making good decisions."

A Journey of Faith

The Christian life—life in the kingdom of God—is a journey, not an arrival. Each of us is either walking toward the Savior or away from him. It is a pilgrim journey, for we are strangers in this land. The braille-like maps that we had before we became Christians no longer work, and the new maps are often blurred. We need guides who have gone ahead. In the eleventh chapter of the Book of Hebrews the writer tells the stories of many who have gone ahead. Some saw their perseverance result in victory. Abraham, Moses, and a host of saints found "success." But many others didn't. They remained in jail. They suffered persecution without relief. They died for their hope. The stories of their journeys are our guides. The conclusion of all the stories is found in the first three verses of chapter 12:

> Therefore, since we are surrounded by such a great cloud of witnesses, let us throw off everything that hinders and the sin that so easily entangles, and let us run with perseverance the race marked out for us. Let us fix our eyes on Jesus, the author and perfecter of our faith, who for the joy set before him endured the cross, scorning its shame, and sat down at the right hand of the throne of God. Consider him who endured such opposition from sinful men, so that you will not grow weary and lose heart.

Kingdom Life

How are we to understand the Christian life? How can we best describe this life in the kingdom of God? What does that mean? How can there be a kingdom, and how can we be citizens of it? If we miss this understanding, we miss the fullness of the life that is called Christian.

Rather than move all around the Bible for an understanding of the Christian life, let us walk through the Gospel of Matthew. After telling us about the birth of Jesus and his family's settling in Nazareth, Matthew introduces us to John the Baptist, who introduces the idea of a kingdom: "In those days John the Baptist came, preaching in the Desert of Judea and saying, 'Repent, for the kingdom of heaven is near!'" (3:1–2).

Next, having told us about the baptism and temptation of Jesus and the imprisonment of John, Matthew moves into the story of Jesus' early ministry: "From that time on Jesus began to preach, 'Repent, for the kingdom of heaven is near.' . . . Jesus went throughout Galilee, teaching in their synagogues, *preaching the good news of the kingdom*, and healing every disease and sickness among the people" (4:17, 23, italics mine).

This kingdom was first announced by John the Baptist and then by Jesus. Their listeners did not understand what they were saying. Because many thought it was an earthly, political kingdom, Jesus had a lot of teaching to do. He preached, announced, and proclaimed "There is *good news*! The kingdom of God has arrived!"

I have chosen to follow one Gospel writer's account, to let him tell the story in his own Spirit-led way. If you were Matthew writing a firsthand account of the life of Jesus, what would you choose to tell your readers about next? Matthew chose to tell us about Jesus' teaching about life in the kingdom:

> Now when he saw the crowds, he went up on a mountainside and sat down. His disciples came to him, and he began to teach them, saying: Blessed are the poor in spirit, for theirs is the kingdom of heaven. . . . Blessed are those who are persecuted because of righteousness, for theirs is the kingdom of heaven (5:1–3, 10).

What a backward, upside down idea! This kingdom was for the poor, the dispirited, the persecuted. But what wonderful news for them!

Qualities of Kingdom Citizens

But there is a great deal more to learn and apply. Jesus describes us as the salt of the earth, a light in the world, a people whose good deeds should be such that others will praise the Father in heaven (5:13–16). Then Jesus offers us an entirely new understanding of how we who are citizens of this kingdom are to act: Don't keep anger against a brother (5:21–26). Don't even think about committing adultery (5:27–31). Keep that binding promise we make in our marriage vows (5:31–32). Do what we say we will do, committing ourselves with a simple "yes" or "no" (5:33–37). Go an extra mile when asked to go only one (5:38–42). Don't only love our neighbors, who may love us, but love our enemies! (5:43–48). Don't give to the needy so that others will think well of us, but give to the needy so our Father, the Ruler of this kingdom, will be pleased with us (6:1–4). When we pray or fast, do it as unto the Lord, not to make points with our spiritual peers (6:5–18). Recognize that we are citizens of one kingdom while living in another; when we think about "profit," we should think about a savings account in the kingdom of heaven rather than in the kingdom of this world (6:19–24).

And because we are citizens of the kingdom of God, we know that there is no need to worry. Our heavenly Father, the Creator of the Universe, is concerned about us! (6:25–34).

An easy task? Jesus didn't think so:

> Enter through the narrow gate. For wide is the gate and broad is the road that leads to destruction, and many enter through it. But small is the gate and narrow the road that leads to life, and only a few find it . . . Not everyone who says to me "Lord, Lord," will enter the kingdom of heaven, but only he who does the will of my Father who is in heaven. Many will say to me on that day, "Lord, Lord, did we not prophesy in your name, and in your name drive out demons and perform many miracles?" Then will I tell them plainly, "I never knew you. Away from me, you evildoers!" (7:13–14, 21–23).

How easy it is to deceive ourselves. The broad path seems so much easier, and if we do good things along the way, especially in the name of Jesus, isn't that enough? Evidently not. Entrance into the kingdom requires discipline.

Demonstrating the Kingdom

But Matthew has more to instruct us. After telling us how Jesus demonstrated his authority through many miracles, he tells us how Jesus went about his ministry by repeating and reinforcing what we heard before: "Jesus went through all the towns and villages, teaching in their synagogues, preaching the good news of the kingdom and healing every disease and sickness" (9:35).

Jesus then commissions and sends forth twelve disciples to proclaim the good news: "As you go, preach this message: 'The kingdom of heaven is near.' Heal the sick, raise the dead, cleanse those who have leprosy, drive out demons" (10:7–8).

Notice the connection between pronouncement and action. Don't just *tell* people. Demonstrate God's power! This was the way Jesus responded to John the Baptist, who in the midst of his prison experience began to doubt and sent his disciples to Jesus:

> When John heard in prison what Jesus was doing, he sent his disciples to ask him, "Are you the one who is to come, or should we expect someone else?" Jesus replied, "Go back and report to John what you hear and see: The blind receive sight, the lame walk, those who have leprosy are cured, the deaf hear, the dead are raised, and the good news is preached to the poor" (11:2–5).

It was action that demonstrated the validity of the words.

The kingdom was not something that would come someday in the future. It had already broken into history. When Jesus was accused by the Pharisees of casting out demons by using the power of Beelzebub, the prince of demons, he replied:

> "Every kingdom divided against itself will be ruined, and every city or household divided against itself will not stand. If Satan drives out Satan, he is divided against himself. How then can his kingdom stand? And if I drive out demons by Beelzebub, by whom do your people drive them out? So then they will be your judges. But if I drive out demons by the spirit of God *then the kingdom of God has come upon you*" (12:25–28, italics mine).

The kingdom was here! When they saw Jesus, they were seeing God at work in the world.

Matthew then records many of Jesus' parables about life in the kingdom:

It is like a man who sowed good seed in his field. But while everyone was sleeping, his enemies came and sowed weeds among the seed and went away (13:24–30). The citizens of the kingdom will live and die among citizens of this world.

It is like a mustard seed, which is very small, but grows so big that birds can light in its branches (13:31–32). It spreads throughout the world like yeast spreads through a loaf of bread (13:33).

It is of immeasurable worth, like finding a treasure hidden in a field or finding a pearl so beautiful that it is worth selling all to acquire it (13:44–46).

Relationships in the Kingdom

Relationships between people in the kingdom of God *are* upside down from the way they are in this world. The disciples asked Jesus, "Who's the greatest in the kingdom of heaven?"

> He called a little child and had him stand among them. And he said: "I tell you the truth, unless you change and become like little children, you will never enter the kingdom of heaven. Therefore, whoever humbles himself like this child is the greatest in the kingdom of heaven" (18:2–4).

That may be one of the most "integrating" statements about kingdom life. What are little children like? Innocent. Trusting. Responsive. Ingenuous. *Real.* They don't play roles unknowingly. They are whole. If we could bring those characteristics to all our relationships, what a difference it would make!

People of power, people with a material view of life, will find this next kingdom principle difficult to understand and accept:

> "I tell you the truth, it is hard for a rich man to enter the kingdom of heaven. Again I tell you, it is easier for a camel to go through the eye of a needle than for a rich man to enter the kingdom of God" (19:23–24).

An Invitation and a Command

God desires that all become citizens of his kingdom. The invitation has been made. It is up to us to respond. Jesus explains this with an analogy:

"The kingdom of heaven is like a king who prepared a wedding banquet for his son. He sent his servants to those who had been invited to the banquet to tell them to come, but they refused to come" (22:2–3).

While the kingdom is growing, spreading like yeast through dough, like the good seed in the field, while it waits discovery like a pearl of great price, the day will come when it will arrive in all its glory and there will be an end to this present age:

"And this gospel of the kingdom will be preached in the whole world, as a testimony to all nations, and then the end will come. . . .They will see the Son of Man coming on the clouds of the sky, with power and great glory. . . .Therefore keep watch, because you do not know on what day your Lord will come" (24:14, 30, 42).

Because we are living citizens of God's kingdom and that the kingdom will have a culmination, we need not only to be ready but also to use wisely the gifts we have been given. The familiar story of the master who left his three servants with five, two, and one talents says it well (25:14–28).

After telling of Jesus' crucifixion, death, and resurrection, Matthew concludes with a meeting between Jesus and his remaining eleven disciples:

Then Jesus came to them and said, "All authority in heaven and on earth has been given to me. Therefore go and make disciples of all nations, baptizing them in the name of the Father and of the Son and of the Holy Spirit, and teaching them to obey everything I have commanded you. And surely I am with you always, to the very end of the age" (28:18–20).

All too often we look at this "Great Commission" and see it merely as a command to tell people the good news. When we think that way, we miss the beginning and the end. The beginning announces that *all authority* has been given to Jesus. Throughout Matthew's whole account there have been continual confrontations with the authority of the Jewish leaders and with Satan. Jesus is now announcing that all authority has been given to him, and it is this authority that empowers us to do what he commands. Do we want authority and power? It is available to us because Jesus has it all and offers it to us. Business may offer authority and power, but it is a different kind. Jesus' power enables us to "glorify God and enjoy him forever."

At the other end we find this statement that Jesus will be with us "to the very end of the age." We are to go forth in power, his power. We are to go forth knowing that he goes with us.

But what is it that he has commanded us to do? How are we to "make disciples of all nations?" We are to baptize them in the name of the Father, the Son, and the Holy Spirit. Just as importantly, we are to teach them to obey. What is it they are to obey? "Everything that I have commanded you." And what he has commanded us is what the Gospel of Matthew is all about: He has commanded us to live as citizens of a new kingdom, the kingdom of God.

Changing the Definition of Success

We are beginning to get a different picture of what it means to be successful. The Jews were waiting for a success that would arrive when they were back on top of the heap, the reestablishment of the kingdom of David. They wanted to be in charge of their lives again and longed for the good old days. They weren't opposed to power. They just wanted that power in their own hands, both individually and corporately. That's what the world affirms. That's what most of American culture is all about. That's what American culture (and too often American Christianity) calls "success." If that is your definition of success, the kingdom is not for you.

How can we exchange our internalized understanding of success and absorb these kingdom values? In attempting to explain how change takes place within us, psychologists and social scientists use a model of knowledge, attitude, behavior, and relationships. Knowledge modifies our attitude about something by changing what we believe, what we say we "know." A change in attitude brings about a change in behavior, the way we act. Changing the way we act has a direct bearing on our relationships with other people, because it is only through observation and experience of what we do that others conclude who we really are.

The Bible anticipates psychology and social science. It talks about the need to have our minds renewed, transformed (Rom. 12:1–2). The "mind" includes what we know at a conscious level, as well as what goes on unconsciously. It includes all those "tapes" that have been programmed into us, for good and for bad. It includes what we feel: our "attitudes." Becoming active citizens of the kingdom of God is a matter of opening our minds to what God would teach us. As we do that, we will redefine for ourselves the meaning of "success." Yes, we will still discover there is a race to be run. There is a competition, but it is not a competition against "flesh and blood" (Eph. 5:12). It is against "principalities and powers," against Satan himself. It is a competition that has already been won for us. Can we win? Yes, we can, because Christ has done it for us.

A few pages back I referred to that special passage from the Sermon on the Mount where Jesus tells us that the reason we don't need to worry about our many needs is that God knows what we need and that he is prepared to give us all we need. The key is the promise in Matthew 6:33: "But seek first his *kingdom* and his righteousness, and all these things will be given to you as well." Notice that the kingdom is in parallel with righteousness: doing right, doing good. The kingdom has rules, but its essence lies in its king and the perfect love he embodies.

Reflections

1. Look through this chapter and make a list of kingdom values.
2. How do the values of the kingdom of God differ from what you have heard about the Christian life?
3. In what ways do these kingdom values diverge from your business values?
4. To the extent that they are different, what aspects of kingdom life will help you let the values of the kingdom predominate at work?

5. If you tried to work out kingdom values in your life, how would that change your definition of success?

Part 3

Making the Story Different

The time has come to write a new story about the rest of your life. Before you do that you need to establish in your own mind the basic rules of living: God's rules.

We find those rules in both the Old and New Testaments. The Old Testament lays a foundation with the Ten Commandments. Jesus summed up the Law by telling us to love God with all our heart and mind and soul and to love our neighbor as ourself. In applying the Ten Commandments to today's world we ask: Is it good? Is it loving? Does it put God first? Does it lead to an integrated life?

When we have dealt with these realities, we are ready to complete our journey by describing for ourselves a successful life.

Values to Live By

Jesus replied: "'Love the Lord your God with all your heart and with all your soul and with all your mind.' This is the first and greatest commandment. And the second is like it: 'Love your neighbor as yourself.' All the Law and the Prophets hang on these two commandments" (Matt. 22:37–40).

How can we live differently? How can we find a new integration between our understanding of success and the reality of the business world?

We have looked at the forces that are at work in the world. We asked the question, "What is success?" And we discovered that our views of success are shaped by a variety of external forces which began at birth and continue today. Our parents, our society, our schools define success. If we live up to these standards, then supposedly we are successful. However, we can experience ourselves as successful only when *we* think we are successful.

We asked the question "What is business?" We analyzed the history of business and how today's business world impacts our thinking. We looked at a number of ways that situations in business conflict with our accepted Christian values.

We defined faith as something more than what we believe. The Bible describes faith as what we do and refuses to separate belief from behavior. But Americans have a unique ability to separate belief from action, and many Christians do the same.

We examined today's American workplace. The invention of money and the Industrial Revolution worked to compartmentalize our lives and pushes us into playing different roles.

We surveyed eight basic "American" values: pluralism, equality, individualism, materialism, competition, capitalism, the notion that each generation is better than the last, and civil religion. These are the values which often stand over against those which we would like to live out as Christians.

We traced the history of the American church. We saw how it too has been shaped by culture.

We looked at today's Christian and set forth the idea of "faith maturity." We noted that American Christians vary from the extremes of a propositional Christianity (beliefs) to a performance Christianity (action). What we need is a balance.

We turned to the question of life in God's kingdom. It is a kingdom that has arrived and is yet to come. It is an upside down kingdom whose values are quite different from the world's.

That's the background. So what are we going to do about it? What *can* we do about it?

Before we can write a new life story, a different story, we need to know what values it should include. Jesus tells us to "'Love the Lord your God with all your heart and with all your soul and with all your mind.' This is the first and greatest commandment. And the second is like it: 'Love your neighbor as yourself.' All the Law and the Prophets hang on these two commandments" (Matt. 22:37–40). The Law of Love stands over all of our decisions. But to understand God's basic definition of how we are to live, we need to look at his basic laws.

The Ten Commandments

Few of us realize how many of our modern laws are based on the Ten Commandments and to what extent they are the ways and means of Western society.

A year or so after *peristroika* a member of the Soviet Academy of Science approached World Vision for help. Over sixty years of communism had demonstrated its inability to provide a soul for the nation. Now the Soviets wanted to discover a set of values on which they could build a new society. The Academy of Science had proposed that they use the Ten Commandments as a yardstick against which to measure current Soviet values. Could World Vision help? We could and we did, but the point is made. Ten laws, given to us over three thousand years ago, are just as fresh and vital as the day God delivered them to Moses, even though to some churches the Ten Commandments may seem rather old-fashioned.

Many Christians say that they are "free from the law," "free in Christ." And yet Jesus' view was that every jot and tittle of the law must be fulfilled (Matt. 5:17–18 KJV). What was the basis of "the law"? Let's look at each one as a beginning for a basic set of values that will work for all of life:

"And God spoke all these words:
'I am the LORD your God,
who brought you out of Egypt,
out of the land of slavery'" (Exod. 20:1–17).

Go Hard after God

"You shall have no other gods before me."

We live in a world of many other religions. In sheer numbers Islam and Hinduism are not far behind Christianity. In the United States we see the continual invention of new religions. New Age would have us to believe that we are gods ourselves and can personally find harmony with the universe. Strange mixtures of Christianity and other self-help movements abound. Because we are a pluralistic society, it goes against the grain to claim that any one religion is more important or more "true" than any other. But the primary Christian value is that God is and that he is the only God. All other gods are false. Only in directing our worship to him, acknowledging him, praying to him, looking to him for sustenance and guidance does life have meaning.

My friend Ray Ortlund, who was also my pastor for many years, has an expression: "Go hard after God!" I would offer that as a primary rule for living. Don't try to nail that down to a strict definition. Whatever it means to *you* is what's important. God knows you. You know God. Go hard after him. Just asking how to do that will bring a whole new understanding of how you should live. True, that understanding may change with time. But God knows all about that too.

Put God first! Go hard after God!

Look Out for Idols

> *"You shall not make for yourself an idol in the form of anything in heaven above or on the earth beneath or in the waters below. You shall not bow down to them or worship them; for I, the LORD your God, am a jealous God, punishing the children for the sin of the fathers to the third and fourth generation of those who hate me, but showing love to a thousand generations of those who love me and keep my commandments."*

The Israelites had a problem. They had a need to see God, to have the assurance that he was right there. When the Ten Commandments were given to Moses on Mount Sinai, the children of Israel had the daily presence of the cloud by day and the fire by night to assure them of God's presence (Exod. 13:21). What more did they need? When the Israelites looked around to see what the other nations were doing, what kind of gods they had, they saw gods made by human hands, gods of wood and stone, creatures of their own imaginations. Sound familiar?

An idol is anything which replaces our focus on God. Money and wealth can be idols:

"People who want to get rich fall into temptation and a trap and into many foolish and harmful desires that plunge men into ruin and destruction" (1 Tim. 6:9).

"For the love of money is a root of all kinds of evil. Some people, eager for money, have wandered from the faith and pierced themselves with many griefs" (1 Tim. 6:10).

"Do not store up for yourselves treasures on earth, where moth and rust destroy, and where thieves break in and steal. But store up for yourselves treasures in heaven, where moth and rust do not destroy, and where thieves do not break in and steal. For where your treasure is, there your heart will be also" (Matt. 6:19–21).

Jesus did not condemn all wealth. He was a middle-class carpenter who had middle-class businessmen as his disciples. He spent time with the rich. But he understood the power of wealth to distract us from our central focus.

Work can serve as an idol. Since business can give us prestige, power, and identity, it can easily absorb our energies. We want to be on the "fast track." It feels good to be able to make decisions that will have a significant impact on the future. It's fun! It is right here. God is somewhere "out there." The challenge of winning the game in business is very tangible.

You can become your own idol. Individualism puts you at the center of the universe. The world rotates around you. That happens when you privatize your faith by not sharing it, when you design your own.

What are your idols? There are big ones and small ones. An idol is anything that consistently takes you away from focusing on God and your neighbor. The idols of the people surrounding the Israelites were fashioned of wood or gold or stone. Ours are much more subtle.

What are yours?

Honor the Lord's Name

> *"You shall not misuse the name of the LORD your God, for the LORD will not hold anyone guiltless who misuses his name."*

There are many ways to misuse the Lord's name. The most obvious is the world's everyday practice of using it as a swear word. For some reason invoking the name "Jesus Christ" is recognized in the English language as being something beyond the pale. To use that name in a derogatory way is to say, "This is so important that I am breaking one of society's rules and using the name of God in vain." But there are other ways to misuse the name of God. We can blame him for our problems. We can use him as a talisman when we are in trouble (foxhole Christianity). We can use him as an excuse. To refuse to misuse God's name is to stand over against a society that sees this as common practice.

We bear the name "Christian." It is an honorable name. It means "Christ's ones." Whenever we dishonor ourselves, we dishonor the name. Whenever we sin against a fellow human being, we misuse the name we have been given.

Take It Easy

"Remember the Sabbath day by keeping it holy. Six days you shall labor and do all your work, but the seventh day is a Sabbath to the LORD your God. On it you shall not do any work, neither you, nor your son or daughter, nor your manservant or maidservant, nor your animals, nor the alien within your gates. For in six days the LORD made the heavens and the earth, the sea, and all that is in them, but he rested on the seventh day. Therefore the LORD blessed the Sabbath day and made it holy."

In the words of Richard Foster, "The fourth commandment strikes at the heart of this everlasting itch to get ahead. We find it so very hard to rest when, by working, we can get a jump on everyone else. There is no greater need today than to lay down the heavy burden of getting ahead."[1]

I am a typical Type A personality. I always have a list of things to get done. I plan ahead, think ahead. I want to see this job done so that I can get on with the next one. So I need people to come alongside me and remind me that this is God's world, and he wants us to enjoy it and enjoy him. Unless we regularly put time aside to focus on God, to "waste time" with him, some other idol has taken his place.

The idea of a Sabbath rest is a difficult one to get hold of in an age when supermarkets are open seven days a week, twenty-four hours a day. Our technology is such that we believe we can't shut anything down for one day. There are power stations to be run, policing to do, food to be served. Many businesses are structured so that even though work is not regularly scheduled over weekends, it is assumed that when something important comes up, work will be done. To refuse to work on Sunday is seen as strange.

It is hard to figure out whether keeping Sunday as the Sabbath is a cultural habit. Many would argue that the concept of setting aside a special time to just know the Lord is the important thing. If we have to work Sundays, then choose another time to spend with God.

The basic idea here is that by putting our work aside in the Lord's name, we are demonstrating our confidence that he will get it done. No need to worry. God *is* in charge.

Is there a place for "God time" on your calendar?

Relationships!

"Honor your father and your mother, so that you may live long in the land the LORD your God is giving you."

God sees people as families, as a unit, as a whole. The unity of the family is maintained because the children of each generation honor their parents. Relationships are of more importance than any other behaviors. The greatest commandment is that we love the Lord and the second is that we love our neighbors. Of all of our "neighbors," our families are of primary importance.

When business takes precedence over family, we are breaking the rules. Some will of course, immediately reply, "But I *work* for my family!" Of course, you do. But that is just one thing that you give them. If money and material things become a substitute for your personal time, you are not caring for your family.

Why should we honor our parents? The obvious reason is for all the things they have done for us. The biblical idea is deeper. Israelite parents were the primary value givers. They recited the law of God to their children. They set examples of worship. They gave their lives to God first. To honor father and mother is to honor what they stand for.

In this day of "dysfunctional families," a time when we experience the need for support groups for children of alcoholic or abusive parents, honoring our parents may seem like a strange idea. But God is the God of Abraham, Isaac, and Jacob, fathers who had a few problems of their own with their children. It is the "faith of our fathers, holy faith" that we sing about. We assume that we stand in a continuous line of saints who have gone before us. When our parents don't seem to be models of such behavior, we can only turn to others who have. So we honor the relationship. We affirm that we are a part of those who have gone before us. We assume that when we become parents, we will pass on the same values, the same ideals, the same love of God.

If you have a family, what values will you pass on to your children? This is no easy challenge. But secular and Christian writers have been dealing with the question of what Gordon Dalby calls *Healing of the Masculine Soul*. Robert Bly, in a more secular book, examines the same phenomenon in *Iron John: A Book About Men*. Both authors decry the loss of what they perceive to be a vital masculinity that is part of the male psyche. Although they do not call us back to the macho man of twenty years ago, they see the erosion of what it means to be a man in our society and encourage men to discover their masculinity, even as women are discovering their femininity.

Preserve Life

"You shall not murder."

Does murder have anything to do with business? Obviously, if your business is a part of the arms industry, you have a much closer connection between business and murder than someone who is in a service business. Murder is different from other forms of killing. Until Christ returns, we will always have wars. There will always be the need for some people to be policemen or soldiers. But murder is taking something away from a person which you had no right to take. It is the ultimate insult.

The 1991 movie *Class Action* told the story of an automobile company which discovered during test procedures on a turning signal that if the car was rear-ended while the left turning signal was operating, an explosion would occur. They had their statisticians calculate how often this was likely to happen. Factually, it was demonstrated that this would happen no more than 160 times for the thousands of cars that would be built. The company's management weighed the $50 million cost of recalling the cars and repairing them against the cost of law suits on behalf of those who were hurt or killed and concluded that liability suits would cost no more than $30 million. They opted not to fix the problem. That was murder.

Stay Pure

"You shall not commit adultery."

Working side-by-side with people day after day can be a friend-ship-building exercise. As more and more women share equal jobs with men, the camaraderie that was once found primarily among men in an earlier day now exists between men and women. And there *is* a big difference in camaraderie between those of the same sex and those of the opposite sex. The natural attraction that men and women have for one another easily develops into intimacy. Obviously, our ability to handle this varies. It becomes increasingly more difficult if we are asked to work overtime together, travel together, be in situations where "no one will ever know" what we have done together.

I am amazed at God's creativity! Certainly sexual intercourse is one of the most exciting experiences of life. You can look at it in two ways: You can simply say that it is built into human nature to procreate and people the earth. Or you can say that it is a reward for that ultimate lifetime promise made to a husband or a wife.

For that reason adultery is potentially the most destructive of all sins. It violates a lifelong promise. It violates another person. It violates us. It strikes at the core of human relationships and stands as the symbol for the disruption of all human relationships. It is the metaphor God used when he condemned Israel for its unfaithfulness. Adultery is the ultimate breaking of a promise or a covenant.

Don't do it. Don't let your business life tempt you into it.

Is It Yours?

"You shall not steal."

When is "good business" really stealing? If a competitor has a good idea and puts it on the market, should we not build on that idea if we see a way of making it better? Sound all right? Suppose we learn quite by chance that a competitor has an idea for a new product, one which will be in direct competition with something we have? Is it all right to use that knowledge?

We suspect that a competitor is working on an improved version of an earlier project. We decide to hire away one of the engineers working on the project at a much increased salary. Is that stealing?

In the same situation, we hire an investigator to secretly discover what is going on in a competitor's laboratory. Stealing?

What we see here is a continuum of situations in which we take something that was not originally ours and use it. Each person must decide in his or her mind what constitutes stealing. It is one of the toughest temptations we face in the business world. We may find it impossible to even think of stealing from our family or friends. But business offers anonymity and impersonal situations where apparently no one gets hurt.

When in doubt, don't!

Don't Damage Your Neighbor

"You shall not give false testimony against your neighbor."

Note that this commandment does not say "Do not lie." Lying is just as sinful as murder (Rom. 1:29–30). But the worst kind of lie is one in which you damage another person, and perhaps this is the lie of which we are all the most guilty. Gossip is its most prevalent form. In the workplace we call it the "grapevine." We pick up half-truths about a person and repeat them as facts to other people. We generalize from one small incident to something like "Well, isn't that just like Jake." "I see that Mary is at it again."

False testimony comes in even more subtle forms. People are quoted to you as having a certain opinion about you or about something else.

In reality it was never said; the person was just trying to make a point. However, it is giving false testimony as to what others have said. In business people continually look for some advantage, and if that makes an outside competitor or one of our rivals inside the company look less than good, so much the better. We disparage a competitor's product. We imply we do it right, but they do it wrong. That's giving a false witness because we are claiming to know something about another person when we don't.

Be Satisfied with What You Have

"You shall not covet your neighbor's house. You shall not covet your neighbor's wife, or his manservant or maidservant, his ox or donkey, or anything that belongs to your neighbor."

The New Testament says this even more succinctly:

Then he [Jesus] said to them, "Watch out! Be on your guard against all kinds of greed; a man's life does not consist in the abundance of his possessions" (Luke 12:15).

What causes fights and quarrels among you? Don't they come from your desires that battle within you? (James 4:1).

You want something but don't get it. You kill and covet, but you cannot have what you want. You quarrel and fight. You do not have, because you do not ask God (James 4:1–2).

Years ago we called it "Keeping up with the Joneses," that desire to look as good, be as well off, and have as much fun as the neighbors down the street or next door. Advertising works all the time on this great desire to have what somebody else has. How insidious it is. Just when we think we have purchased the car of our dreams or redone our house to the family's satisfaction, our co-worker drives into the parking lot with a slightly better car than we felt we could afford or invites us to his completely remodeled and professionally decorated home.

That's what many businesses are about—convincing potential customers that they *need* a certain product or service. Do they? I remember a World Vision staff member who had been overseas for many years. After his return he walked through a Southern California shopping mall. He was convinced that no more than 20 percent of the items on sale were really needed by anyone!

But isn't that what our society is based on? Don't we need to keep finding better products, more efficient ways to live? It takes very little thought to know the correct answer. A few people, like the Pennsylvania Amish, have cried "Enough!" They decided to opt for simplicity by locking their society in time. No automobiles. No power tools. Simple clothes. Simple ways. Happy people. They have much to teach us.

To not covet is to be satisfied. Hear that! All those things that we talked about in chapter 1, things that program a warped concept of success into us, fall into this wanting to be as good as or better than we perceive someone else to be.

Working out Values

Stating Our Values

In years past the differences between denominations was based on "doctrinal distinctives." As we noted in chapter 6, those distinctives are becoming less and less important to American Christians. That is not necessarily bad. But a local church that has no way of defining what is sinful and what is not, what is important and what is not, what it will die for and what it will not, is not able to provide guidance to its members as they seek to work out their lives in business.

It does not follow that every local church should have identical distinctives. A church must deal with its local culture, must attempt to distinguish among the good, the bad, and the neutral in that culture and corporately define its primary values in that culture. That is not easy in an America which holds up pluralism as an ideal. The non-Christian community, and perhaps even the Christian community, may think such distinctives are strange. I know I have felt that way. When a local church in Southern California publicly told its members not to associate with a person who refused to repent, I judged that too harsh. Later I realized that the church needed to do that to enforce its stated values.

Core Values

Unfortunately, churches tend to think only in terms of statements of faith and/or bylaws that produce a set of rules. Rules assume compliance. They are answers to questions we think will be asked, but they can never cover every situation. I would encourage every church to also write a set of core values. Such values are ideals toward which we work rather than absolutes to which we adhere. I will refer to The Core Value Statement of World Vision International, a multinational Christian relief and development agency. World Vision's core values encompass six areas: *We are Christian. We are committed to the poor. We value people. We are stewards. We are partners. We are responsive.* For the sake of brevity, I will quote only the "We are Christian" section:

> We acknowledge one God, Father, Son and Holy Spirit. In Jesus Christ the love, mercy and grace of God are made known to us and all people. From this overflowing abundance of God's love we find our call to ministry.

> We proclaim together, "Jesus lived, died, and rose again. Jesus is Lord." We desire him to be central in our individual and corporate lives.

> We seek to follow him——in his identification with the poor, the afflicted, the oppressed, the marginalized; in his special concern for children; in his respect for the dignity bestowed by God on women equally with men; in his challenge to unjust attitudes and systems; in his call to share resources with each other; in his love for all people without discrimination or conditions; in his offer of new life through faith in him. From him we derive our holistic understanding of the gospel of the Kingdom of God, which forms the basis of our response to human need.

We hear his call to servanthood and see the example of his life. We commit ourselves to a servant spirit permeating the organization. We know this means facing honestly our own pride, sin and failure.

We bear witness to the redemption offered through faith in Jesus Christ. The staff we engage are equipped by belief and practice to bear this witness. We will maintain our identity as Christian, while being sensitive to the diverse contexts in which we express that identity.

World Vision doesn't claim that its personnel are to be living up to all these values at all times and in every situation. Rather, it holds up these values as being desirable.

The Old Testament laid out the basics. The New Testament talks about living a different life because we have been incorporated into a kingdom. If we are going to live a life that is successful in our eyes and God's eyes, then we need to find a way to interpret what life in the kingdom of God in *this* day, in *this* place, and in *these* circumstances might be like. The temptation is to search for a set of do's and don'ts—rules—that we can apply to each situation. We would like a set of instructions to go with each new challenge. But rules don't work that way. Rules that were just fine a year ago no longer seem to fit. The kingdom of God has certain built-in principles that we expect will lead to values we hold. From these values we will find rules to apply to given situations. The values we hold and the rules we apply make up our ethics.

Even if I live by all my values, it does not necessarily follow that I will be satisfied that I am successful. Indeed, I could become a very embittered person. I could picture myself as a martyr, the only one who is doing right. I also *need* the approval of others. Values that are not derived in the midst of relationships are just personal opinions.

Finding Values in Relationships

For the Christian, success is based on the conviction that we have a relationship with the most important being in the universe, God Almighty. That alone is adequate for a few people, but not for most. We experience God's affirmation in the affirmation of people like ourselves, people whose opinions we value. That is what the church is all about. From the "cloud of witnesses" that have gone before (Heb. 12:1) and those with whom we have everyday fellowship, we discover the needed assurance that we are all right. God intends the local church to be a living demonstration that the kingdom of God has arrived and is in our midst. Success has to be measured first in terms of our relationship with others. Without that fellowship there is no measure of success.

The apostle James sums up that principle this way:

> Is any one of you in trouble? He should pray. Is anyone happy? Let him sing songs of praise. Is any one of you sick? He should call the elders of the church to pray over him and anoint him with oil in the name of the Lord. And the prayer offered in faith will make the sick person well; the Lord will raise him up. If he has sinned, he will be forgiven. Therefore confess your sins to each other and pray for each other so that you may be healed. The prayer of a righteous man is powerful and effective. . . . My brothers, if one of you should wander from the truth and someone should bring him back, remember this: Whoever turns a sinner from the error of his way will save him from death and cover over a multitude of sins (James 5:13–16, 19–20).

You need to share your life with others, testing the quality of your life not only by others' verbal agreement, but also by living out your life in a community. If you are reading this book alone, again let me encourage you to find a group of others to share it with.

Love God and Do as You Please

"Love God and do as you please." These words of St. Augustine probably hit every seminary student pretty much the same way. "Do as you please!" Why, I'd love to do as I please, especially if it didn't get me into trouble! The counterbalance is, of course, "love God." But how do I know I love God?

> A new command I give you: Love one another. As I have loved you, so you must love one another. By this all men will know that you are my disciples, if you love one another (John 13:34–35).

> This is how we know what love is: Jesus Christ laid down his life for us. And we ought to lay down our lives for our brothers. If anyone has material possessions and sees his brother in need but has no pity on him, how can the love of God be in him? Dear children, let us not love with words or tongue but with actions and in truth (1 John 3:16–18).

> Dear friends, since God so loved us, we also ought to love one another (1 John 4:11).

Loving God is the greatest value of all. That love is demonstrated by loving our brothers and sisters.

Based on what we looked at in chapter 6, that is not the normal experience of most Christians in most local churches. Being a Christian is a radical idea. It implies a sharp right-hand turn from the way our society would tell us to live. A radical Christian community is one that must stand at a distance from its culture lest it be overwhelmed by that culture. To keep that from happening, there needs to be a set of values that each local church holds as its own.

Notice how this understanding of the extreme importance of a worshiping community that James describes runs counter to our inbred individualism. When God's Word tells us that "You are no longer your own; you were bought with a price" (1 Cor. 6:19b–20a), it is also telling us that to belong to God is to belong to one another. To belong to one another is to be accountable to one another, even to confess our sins to one another, and to go out and try to bring back the sinner! That's heavy stuff!

Living Out Our Value System

Is It Good?

At one level that is a very simple question. If it is good, then it is permissible. If it is not, then it is not permissible. At another level we have to ask the question "How do we know what good is?" That can be an unnecessary smoke screen.

Good is a very powerful word that we often use quite glibly: "Good for you!" "That's good." But God used it to assess his creation. In Genesis 1:31 we read, "And God saw all that he had made, and it was very good." I think of all the tests we might apply to our actions and our decisions and "*Is it good?*" encompasses a host of other values. If it is good, it is not unjust, dishonest, or harmful.

As our faith matures, each of us has a growing sense of good. Hopefully goodness will permeate more and more of our lives. But right now each of us has an understanding of what we mean by "good." Even if you can only say "I know it when I see it," that is an adequate test. Is this job you are being asked to do *good*? Is this decision you are making good—in the sense that *you* believe it is good?

But can we trust ourselves always to identify good? No. But if we trust the Holy Spirit to help make the decision, then we can trustingly press ahead. Jesus said the Holy Spirit came to "teach us all things" (John 14:26).

Notice how different our ideal values are from rules. They permit us to ask ourselves (and to allow others to ask), "Does this action reflect a core value?"

Is It Loving?

If the word *love* had not become so devalued in our society, we would have put this before "Is it good?" From an ethical point of view, "Is it loving?" always asks the question, "Is it for the better good of other people?" rather than "Is it for *my* good?" Love is an action word.

> Love is patient
> Love is kind
> It does not envy
> It does not boast
> It is not proud
> It is not self-seeking
> It is not easily angered
> It keeps no record of wrongs
> Love does not delight in evil, but rejoices with the truth
> It always protects
> It always trusts
> It always hopes
> It always perseveres (1 Cor. 13:4–7).

Can love work in a business setting? Notice first some of the contrasts built into this familiar quotation from Paul's first letter to the church at Corinth. Patience, kindness, contentment, restraint, and humility are attributes of people who are so secure in who they are that there is no need to compare themselves with others nor make sure others are aware of their success. Only those whose confidence of success is complete can act that way.

The other side of "not delighting in evil" is to rejoice when truth is evident. Jesus said the light of truth exposes the deeds of darkness. It is the loving thing to expose evil because in so doing we hope to keep it from damaging others.

Love protects what? Protects whom? Protects from what? Protects from whom? Certainly from evil. Certainly those whom evil seeks to damage. Love is not naive. It knows all about the evil in the world and stands ready to protect others from that evil.

In what does love trust? It trusts in God's goodness and his justice. For what does it *hope*? In the midst of all the hurt in the world, it sees beyond the will to a better kingdom.

And it perseveres. That's the hardest thing to do. To keep on going in the face of personal defeat, lack of support, and the stress of daily living requires a special gift of grace.

Does It Reflect My Ideal Story?

Each of us "leads" a life. We can look back and say, this is the story of my life. But the story is not ended. There is more to tell. What will it be like? What do you wish it would be like? Each of us needs not only short-term goals, but also an ideal life story. In the chapters that follow we will examine a plan for developing that new, ideal life story.

Your ideal story becomes a primary value for you. If this is what you believe you should be, if this is the future you think is God's best for you, then is this decision, this action going to validate or violate that story: Where will it lead?

Does It Put God Second?

For some reason that is an easier question to answer than, "Does it put God first?" To put God second implies that you know what you are doing and you have compared it to God's best for you and then decided not to opt for his best. At first glance that seems almost impossible. Most of us know it is not!

Does It Lead to an Integrated Life?

The reason that Muslims insist on a government that embodies the teaching of the Koran is that they realize you can't live part of your life "under God" and part of it under some other authority. The early Pilgrims had the same view. Our Constitution dictates a separation between church and state, by which we mean that the state cannot dictate our religion and no single religion can tell the state how to conduct its affairs. Such a division protects us, even as it pushes us away from any religion.

As we saw earlier, there was considerable doubt as to whether such pluralism could work. But it has. And in doing so it has added to the inner pluralism that forces us to play so many roles, roles that have different sets of values. One of our core values must be to apply the same rules to as many aspects of daily living as we can.

Reflections

Throughout this book you have been encouraged to share the experience of answering these reflection questions. Now we come to some very personal questions. If you are able to share these answers with your fellow class members, you are close to a biblical community.

1. What does it mean to you to "Go hard after God"?
2. What are the idols in your life that you may be putting in the place of God?
3. Are there other ways of misusing the name of the Lord besides swearing? Which ones might you be guilty of?

4. Is getting your job done sometimes more important than your relationships? What are some examples of that?

5. Is there a balance between your relationships at home and your relationships at work? Do your family members think so?

6. Are there ways in which your business can harm other people?

7. Are you tempted to have extramarital relationships on the job? What can you do to reduce that temptation?

8. Does your company ever steal anything from others? Do *you* steal anything from your company?

9. Does office gossip or company policy damage people's integrity?

10. What dissatisfactions in your life are related to seeing what other people have? Are they really important? What do you do to satisfy those wants? Is it worth the effort?

11. Does your church have a statement of faith, bylaws, or other descriptions of what its members stand for? Are you able to practice them on the job? If not, why not?

12. In what way has love become or not become your dominant value?

If we are to live out a different story, we need a new vision of the future, a new way of looking at the world, a better place to stand. We can begin by taking seven steps: trust in God, see life as a whole, recognize the roles we play, understand God's values, understand the world's values, write a new story, and act.

But before we can effectively take those steps we need to establish intimate communication with God, and we have to find other members of the body of Christ to support us.

10

Moving into the Future

You live in an inner world of powerful images, stories, and pictures of what you would like to be. You started writing that story a long time ago. "When I grow up . . . ." When I grow up—how many times have you felt the realism of that half-humorous question, "What are you going to be when you grow up?" What are you going to do? Where is life leading? What would you like your life to be?

Your life is filled with the images and tapes of your past, and stories of what has gone before. Those images have been shaped by childhood, school, relationships, and most powerfully, by the world you live in. They shape the way you think, the way you feel, the way you act. They are the pushers and shovers that make up your daily story. Some are good. Others are not. But what about a *new* story? What might it look like?

If you are to live a different story, you need a new vision of the future, a new way of looking at the world, a better place to stand. There are many stories to choose from. Many people have gone before.

Many people are living lives that you might want to imitate. The Bible calls us to dream dreams and have visions about a story modeled on a life that was lived out almost two thousand years ago. It's a story about a king and a kingdom, a story about how to live every day in that kingdom.

Every story has a beginning and an ending. When we have read halfway through a good novel, we wonder how it will end. We have images of a happy ending, a better ending, one which will be pleasing. What kind of an ending would you like to your story?

The Context of a Life Story

We have talked about a lot of things. "Success" is very much something of our own imagination and desires. If we want to be more successful as Christians, two things are necessary: First, we have to have a foundation on which to build, one that is based on a common set of values that will work in the office, at home, in church, and in the business world. Second, we need to use that foundation to construct a more integrated life.

The proper foundation for a Christian's life story reflects the values of the "kingdom of God." We are citizens of a kingdom that has different values, different laws, different rules from the world in which we carry on our everyday life. The overarching value is the Law of Love—love of God, love of oneself, and equal love for one's neighbors, not only the people next door, but also "neighbors" at work and in the supermarket and persons we meet only casually. The foundational laws are ten. They are so enduring that through the years Jews and Christians have called these *the* Ten Commandments. Different from the Law of Love, but flowing from it, they are set in both positives and negatives. Positively we are to honor God and our parents. Negatively we are to refrain from setting out after false gods, seeking after things that are not ours or hurting our neighbor by saying untruths about him, stealing from him, robbing him of his life.

There are some specific steps to this process of finding success as a Christian. You may be well along on some and not so far on others:

1. Trust in God.
2. See life as an integrated whole.
3. Recognize the roles you play.
4. Understand God's values.
5. Understand the world's values.
6. Write a new life story.
7. Act.

We will review the first five steps in this chapter and then deal with the others in the final chapters.

Before You Begin

If you are going to be able to take those seven steps, you will need some help. As a Christian you cannot rewrite this story alone. I can't write it alone because it isn't my story. It is *our* story. First, it is Jesus and me. Second, it is the body of Christ and you. The most important part of that body is your family, so it is their story too. But as we saw in chapter 8, life in the kingdom is a life lived in fellowship with others, a fellowship called the church. You need co-authors and editors and perhaps even some scriptwriters to help you. What help can you get?

Find a place to pray. We find our vertical relationship with the Savior through prayer, through his Word, and through the ministry of the Holy Spirit. The first chapter of your new story needs to be written with Jesus so I encourage you to not only have a time of regular prayer, but also a place of regular prayer. My place is a corner of our blue living room couch facing the mantle with its antique clock and painting of a night scene in a Dutch harbor. My time is 6:10 A.M. At that hour the living room is completely mine. In the half-hour there I have time to listen to God through reading his Word and to share with him my praise, my thanksgiving, my faults, and my needs. Perhaps prayer is not easy for you. If you are struggling to communicate with God, let me suggest Bill Hybels' small book, *Too Busy Not to Pray*.

Have a prayer journal. Purchase a bound notebook in which you *write out* your prayers. This can be a scary experience! It takes some courage to *write* what we are really thinking—our real needs, our sins. Suppose someone else reads it? (Thankfully, I have a wife who is a marriage and family counselor, and she knows the need for confidentiality.) Tell your spouse and children that this is a private journal. Begin each day's entry with the date, your location, and the reference to any Scripture you may have read. Then have at it. If you need a special page to remind you of things you should always pray about, fine, but keep your prayer requests current. I take a great deal of joy in writing in the date when a request was answered. Sure, sometimes I have to put an X in front of the request; it wasn't answered the way I hoped. But there really aren't too many of those.

Having such a journal does a number of things. It gives you a record of your consistency in prayer. It gives you assurance that you have been praying, because you can read your prayers back to God! It helps you plot your spiritual journey as it goes. Later I'll suggest how to use the same journal for rewriting your life story.

Look for help from your family. Share with them your desire to write a story that pleases God. Ask for their prayers. After all, if you make a dramatic change in your life, they will be part of that change, just as they are part of your past and present. Maybe this should be a joint story written with your spouse. This can be a humbling experience. It is hard to tell your family, "I am not the person God wants me to be. I need to change." But you know as well as I do that most families are strengthened by discovering that husband and wife, Dad and Mom have feet of clay.

Seek out other Christians. I have said that over and over. It is key. You may already be part of a close fellowship. Perhaps your church has small groups or covenant groups. If there isn't a satisfactory group available, look for another person who might share your dreams and start one. If what I have said about how individualism shapes us into the world's mold is true (and it is!), then no Christian can go it alone.[1]

Seven Steps to Success

With that beginning, let's look at the seven steps in writing a new life story, a different story.

1. *Trust God*

That's really the problem, isn't it? It isn't so much a question of belief as it is of trust. It God really for me? Is God really on *my* side? Can I trust him to do good?

You have probably heard the expression, "Let go, and let God." The implication is that as long as we hold on to ourselves, and don't completely trust God, he can't act on our behalf. You might respond, "*Can't do it? What kind of a God is that? I thought God could do everything.*" Yes, he can, but he is a God who has given us freedom to trust him or not to trust him, a loving God who gives us freedom to love or not to love. Belief is wrapped up in trust. We have to know what it is we trust. We need to believe that God is *for* us.

But there are other aspects to trusting God. Do you believe that God knows everything, that he is omniscient? There are magnificent implications in believing that! If God knows everything we do and still loves us, then he loves us unequivocally, without reservation. On the other hand, if God knows everything we do, we have two motivations for seeking out and doing good. The first is fear. God has built consequences into his world. We violate his commandments at our peril. The second is joy. If God knows everything we do, then he knows the good things we do, affirms them, affirms us.

Believe God's Word, the Bible. There has been much discussion about what that means. Does it mean that we believe the original manuscripts contained no errors of any kind? Perhaps. I personally don't find that notion very helpful, since I have no access to those original manuscripts. Most importantly it means that the Bible I hold in my hand is God's Word for *me* and for you. One of the key doctrines of the church through the centuries has been the doctrine of the preservation of Scripture, the idea that God has seen to it that his Word is preserved for each succeeding generation. We have only to look at the history of the Bible to validate this truth. Beyond that is the superintendence of the Holy Spirit to teach us those things we need to learn as we read, know, and share God's Word with others. Whatever version you hold in your hand—a King James Version, a New American Standard, a New International Version, or one of many others—God uses it to communicate to us. From our belief in God's Word flows all our other understandings.

Believe that God is the only God. The cry of the Jews from antiquity is, "Hear, O Israel, the Lord your God is one God." There are no others. Do you believe that, or have you unconsciously bought into a pluralism that says that what *you* believe is no better than what someone else may believe? To believe that God is the only God is to believe that there are transcendent values, rules, and laws which govern the universe. In Psalm 119 we read of God's Word, his laws, ordinances, statutes, precepts, and decrees. There are no others. All laws of the universe are God's, whether or not humans have discovered them. That is why we should never be surprised when the world stumbles on and applies them and discovers they work. Newton discovered God's law of gravity. Today we are seeing corporations discovering God's law of love.

Believe that God desires a better future for you. If that is true, then you *can* change. You can write a new ending to the story of your life. If God is for you, who can be against you?

What, then, shall we say in response to this? If God is for us, who can be against us? He who did not spare his own Son, but gave him up for us all—how will he not also, along with him, graciously give us all things? Who will bring any charge against those whom God has chosen? It is God who justifies. Who is he that condemns? Christ Jesus, who died—more than that, who was raised to life—is at the right hand of God and is also interceding for us. Who shall separate us from the love of Christ? Shall trouble or hardship or persecution or famine or nakedness or danger or sword? As it is written: "For your sake we face death all day long; we are considered as sheep to be slaughtered." No, in all these things we are more than conquerors through him who loved us. For I am convinced that neither death nor life, neither angels nor demons, neither the present nor the future, nor any powers, neither height nor depth, nor anything else in all creation, will be able to separate us from the love of God that is in Christ Jesus our Lord (Rom. 8:31–39).

Believe that God not only forgives the mistakes of the past, but has forgotten them! That seems impossible at first glance. I can understand how a loving God would forgive my sin as I confessed it to him, but how can a God who knows everything forget my past?

> The LORD is compassionate and gracious, slow to anger, abounding in love. He will not always accuse, nor will he harbor his anger forever; he does not treat us as our sins deserve or repay us according to our iniquities. For as high as the heavens are above the earth, so great is his love for those who fear him; as far as the east is from the west, so far has he removed our transgressions from us (Ps. 103:8–12).

On the basis of all of this believe that God will help you to change. The church has always understood the idea of growing in grace and maturity. God does not want you to remain as a child. He wants you to grow in love and knowledge. No matter how flawed your past may have been, it is his good desire that your future be better, that you be a success.

2. See Life as an Integrated Whole

In our post-Enlightenment world we are continually trying to take things apart, to dissect them, to see what makes them work. The Industrial Revolution broke work down into "logical" components and in so doing we forgot the whole of work and of life. Psychology divides us up. Schools grade us. Sociologists and anthropologists classify us. John Donne's oft-quoted statement that "no man is an island" needs to be preceded by "each person leads a whole life." If we are to be "a part of the main," we have to try to bring all of ourselves to the task. This is not a one-time effort. For every two steps ahead, there will probably be one backward. It is not accomplished by sheer willpower, by taking one's "self" in hand. Rather it is a process where we continually paint an ever-improving picture of the future.

At the moment you may be living many completely differentiated lives. Trying to fit all the pieces together may seem much like mixing up three or four jigsaw puzzles and then trying to make all of the

pieces fit into one whole. It doesn't work. You have to have one uni-
fying picture.

How do you get such a picture? We'll be discussing that in the next
chapter.

3. Recognize the Roles You Play

I have implied in previous chapters that the search for wholeness
begins by first understanding the roles that you play and the dissimi-
lar values you probably apply to those various roles. What are your
roles? Figure 2 is a beginning list to work on. Add to it. Modify it.
Note where you think change is needed.

4. Understand God's Values

God's values are expressed as principles of a unique kingdom. This
kingdom has a king, not a constitutional monarchy such as we find in
Great Britain, but an *absolute* monarchy in which the king rules. This
is the beginning point of understanding the life that is Christian. We
discover this kingdom in a number of ways. In the first chapter of his
letter to the Romans Paul tells us that one way of knowing God is to
look around us: "For since the creation of the world God's invisible
qualities—his eternal power and divine nature—have been clearly
seen, being understood from what has been made, so that men are
without excuse" (Rom. 1:20).

We discover the kingdom in God's Word. In chapter 8 we discussed
what life in God's kingdom was all about. Much of what we discussed
is based on what God's Word says. The Gospels are about a kingdom
that has come and is yet to come and how to live a life in that kingdom. We look to the Bible to reveal God's values and judge everything by the Bible's teachings. If the Bible affirms it, we affirm it. If
the Bible disputes it, so do we. If the Bible remains silent on the matter, we look for the biblical principles that will guide our actions.

We discover the kingdom in the life of the church. The church is not
the kingdom, but it is intended to be a reflection of the kingdom. Certainly it fails continuously, but in the amazing words of Jesus, "The
gates of hell shall not prevail against it" (Matt. 16:18).

Figure 2

Role	Primary Values	Need to Change What?
Head of Family	Concern for family, need for control, family rules, society's rules	
Spouse	Lifetime commitment, caring for one another	
Parent	Concern for children, means of control, deciding what's best for the future	
Child	What the parent wants, what peers are demanding	
Worker	Company's goals, supervisors' requirements, how to get ahead, competition, position, prestige	
Church Member	What others think, biblical norms, church polity and policy	
Christian Witness	What Christ thinks, what other Christians think, what the person being witnessed to will think	
Skier	Enjoyment, competition with self and others	
Friend	Friend's values	
Carpool Driver	Safety, traffic laws	
Shopper	Price, convenience, quality	
Volunteer	Concern for others or for a cause	

What we first learn from the church is the concept of community and how we are to live with each other in Christian fellowship. When we submit ourselves to this community, we submit ourselves to God.

We discover the kingdom as the Holy Spirit ministers to us. Jesus promised that after he was gone, he would send the Comforter, the Holy Spirit, to remind us of all he had said (John 14:26). Paul tells us that we are led by the Spirit (Rom. 8:14). Indeed, when we can't pray for ourselves, the Spirit intercedes for us (Rom. 8:26).

We discover the kingdom as we minister to others. Modern psychology is ahead of us in finding God's ways! Are you despondent, depressed? Find someone who needs help and serve them. Your despondency will disappear, your depression will wane. It is in serving that we are served. It is in giving that we receive. It is in loving that we find love.

5. Understand the World's Values

We understand the world's values best when we see them over against kingdom values, for it is here they stand out in stark relief. It is important to understand how these values come to be. In learning their history (chapters 4 and 5) we find that values change and develop over time. They need not stay the same. We do not have to conform to them. We have seen that we are children of our culture and our society's history. In chapter 5 we looked at seven of the world's values that push us away from seeing God's kingdom values.

Reflections

Before we move on to how we write a new story, try to answer the following questions:

1. Do you really believe God is for you? In what ways have you learned to trust God? What more do you yet have to learn?

2. In what way do the different parts of your life conflict with one another?

3. What roles are you playing? What are the values associated with them. Use the chart on page 187.

4. In what way do the world's values clash with the values you desire?

As you write a new life story, don't be satisfied with "somedays." Step out in faith and write down specific measurable goals that describe what you believe God wants you to be. Begin with the distant future. Fifteen years from now what goals would you like to attain? Work back from those to the present, writing more goals as you come closer and closer.

Share this new story with your spouse or other close friends. Test it against God's Word. When you are satisfied, begin. Act! And as you move into this new future, keep testing and re-evaluating. If it's not the best, change it. Today really is the first day of the rest of your life!

11

Writing a Different Story

We are future-oriented human beings so we all have our "somedays." Someday this will happen. Someday I will get married. Someday I will have children. Someday things will be different. Even in a traditional society where tomorrow is very much the same as today there are "somedays." The Maasai people of Africa are such a people. Within the Maasai culture are "age ranks," composed of every male born within a seven-year span. Each age rank has its place in Maasai society, with the oldest age rank having the authority and responsibility to lead the tribe. Every young man looks forward to the time when he will attain that high position. The Maasai have their "somedays." Their big advantage over us is that they can see the future modeled before them and appreciate what they look forward to. In our society we have many more "somedays," many more possibilities. The difficulty with our "somedays" is that they may be nothing more than a bright illusion.

The Awesome Power of Goals

How do you decide about tomorrow? There is nothing more motivating than clearly defined goals. They give us the ability to take our eyes off the present with all its problems and look ahead to a place where we can see the possibilities of the future. Goals are therapeutic.[1] Psychologists have pointed out how helpful it is to stop dwelling on all the difficulties that surround us today and start imagining what the world would be like if we (and it) were different. There is a difference between "Someday" thinking and goal-thinking. "Someday" by its very nature tends to be fuzzy and undetermined. Goals are specific, measurable objectives that we want to see happen in the future. They have specific dates attached to them. "Someday I am going to visit Indonesia" is quite different from, "I am planning to spend two weeks in Indonesia between January 7 and 21." For most of us too much of our life is wrapped up in indefinite somedays.

For a number of years Ted Engstrom and I taught a seminar titled "Managing Your Time." It was really about how to get control of your life and manage it in a more God-honoring and self-satisfying way, but we wanted to attract mission executives and pastors. We had a rather strong suspicion that if we titled the seminar "Managing Your Life," not many people would come. Over the years we had the privilege of teaching thousands of pastors and Christian workers. During the early years of the seminar we continually sought to improve it, to make our communication better by getting our ideas in order. We finally settled on three things that were needed: *goals*, *priorities*, and *planning*. We need clear goals toward which to move, but the goals we create for ourselves need to be determined by biblical priorities. To realize those goals we need to plan for them. Having done our planning, it is in living them out that we find better goals and higher priorities and learn to make more effective plans.[2] Year after year we have seen people make major changes in their lives because they decided what it was that they wanted to do, set some specific goals to accomplish that, and then did it. You can too!

Goals Come in All Sizes—And They Change

You can set a goal to meet someone for lunch in an hour, to complete a report tonight, or to make sure you help your daughter with her homework. These are specific things that have time boundaries. You can set goals farther out, goals for things like a vacation next summer, selling so much product by June 1, finding a new way of completing testing before the new product comes on line August 10, or hiring a new staff person before the end of a year.

Then there are more distant goals—graduating from college in four years, training for a new job in three years, building a new home in five years. Beyond those, we can describe much longer-term goals, some of which may take a lifetime. To start an effective new ministry to the poor in your community, to own and manage your own business, to rethink, write out, and live out values that reflect a biblical understanding of who and why you are—these are long-term goals.

We mark off our life stories by events—births, graduations, first jobs, marriages, deaths, special vacations, noteworthy accomplishments. Completed goals become the milestones on which we hang our memories. Future goals are milestones for the still-unfinished part of our life's story, what lies ahead. Goals give us a way to communicate with ourselves and with others about how we hope our lives will turn out. Goals are statements of faith for—like any statement about the future—we have no assurance we can reach them. We need to remember with James, the brother of Jesus, that Christian goals are always preceded by "God willing" (see James 4:13–15).

In the revised edition of his *Motivation and Personality*, Abraham Maslow describes what he calls the Grumble Theory. He says that after we have worked very hard to attain a goal, that wonderful euphoria of success doesn't last very long. When we start to think about all that it cost us to accomplish this exceptional thing and wonder whether it was worth all the effort, we discover that success based on accomplishment is a fleeting sensation. An Olympic swimmer trains for years for that wonderful ten days of competition. That day comes. After she not only wins three gold medals and a silver, praise and honor are heaped on her. Everyone wants her autograph. But then what? If another goal does not lie before us, success can turn to ashes in our mouths.

We need a story that carries us into the future. In the words of a gospel song I heard many years ago, we need "eternity's values in view." We need to write that story ahead of time and then try to live it. We need to have vision of a better future. It gives us something to live for, something in our hearts that gets us out of bed in the morning with a smile of anticipation. How do we find such a vision? How do we know it is the *right* vision?

Writing a New Story

Unfortunately too many of us have only a hazy idea of a "desirable" future. We can imagine some nice general possibilities, but we haven't shaped them into specifics. We may have a story line, but the content is missing. How do we find those goals?

To write an ending to a life story, one which brings glory to God, it's necessary to distance yourself from where you are at this moment. You need to project yourself far enough into the future so that your story becomes believable. Very few things can be accomplished in ten days. Almost anything can be accomplished in ten years! But where to begin the writing of this new future? There are many places. You might best begin with your spouse or family or with a group of people who have an equal dissatisfaction with the way their story is playing out. Some people may best do it alone.

Fantasizing in prayer is an excellent starting point. Imagine you are living in the best of all worlds. Good things are happening to you. As you think about that best of all futures, consciously draw yourself into the presence of God. Specifically ask him, "Father, I really would like to bring glory to you. I want to enjoy you not only forever, but also in this life. Open up my mind to that which would be most pleasing to you. And because it's pleasing to you, give me the assurance that it would be pleasing to me also. Thank you, Father."

What kind of life would that be? Get in your mental helicopter and fly over where you are. Where are you living? What are you doing? Are you married, not married? Are your children grown? Perhaps you don't have any children. What does your working day look like? What pleases you? Write down a description of how the best of life might be ten to fifteen years from now. Keep writing. What has happened in this life? Suppose it ended at this imaginary moment fifteen years hence, what would your friends say about you as they remembered you?

Try writing your own obituary. Pretend that you are a reporter digging into the facts. If you accomplished some great thing for God, consider why that happened. What started you on this road? Perhaps you don't see some great "worldly" accomplishment, but rather would like to be remembered as a person who was a helper and a mentor for others. How did that begin?

Now think about how God has made you, gifted you. What talents do you have? What is really fun for you? Fit that into the story. Sometimes we discover that the person we would like to become would really be a drag.

Review what you have written. Is this God's best for you? Pray about it. Think about it. Modify it. Describe your story in terms of some goals: "In fifteen years I want to be teaching in a graduate school and doing consulting." "In fifteen years my goal is to be CEO of a company that has a national reputation for its high-quality products." "In fifteen years I want to be known as a man who loved God." "In fifteen years I see myself living and working as a missionary in an Asian country." State your goals in clear, unambiguous terms.

Now see what values are imbedded in this new and better life. Will this life permit you to live out kingdom values? If not, why not? What would have to change so you could honor those values? Is life beginning to come into focus as a whole? Do you see the roles you play beginning to merge together? Can you see your values as being consistent in them all?

Back from the Future

When you feel comfortable with this (remember that you're not making a lifetime decision, but trying to visualize a better future), take the next step. Move back from the future toward the present. If this is the kind of life you would like to live, what steps must you take in the coming years to make it happen? Would you have to change jobs, or get a different kind of education, or move into a different industry? Would it require retraining? Will you need new personal relationships? Will the quality of your relationships have to change? Perhaps you feel that you're not spiritually or technologically prepared to make the kind of changes that are required. What does that indicate you must do in the next five years? Write that down.

Some of your in-between steps may be five years away. Others may be much closer. The next step is to decide what to do about it today. Where do you begin? What exactly do you do? Who are the other people with whom you need to take this journey? Look at each of those midpoint goals and see which goals you need to achieve in the near future. For example, if you believe you will need an entirely different kind of training in five years, what must you do this year to begin that training?

You can see that the approach we are taking is very "businesslike." Business people are used to thinking about "projecting" into the future, making forecasts, making plans. Unfortunately, too often they don't use those same skills when it comes to their own life or in their families. That's the result of both displaced values and playing different roles with different rules. What particular gifts has God given you that might be useful in thinking through how to plan your future life?

Begin listing the goals (the milestones) for this successful venture! Decide where you want to be five years and fifteen years from now. Plot out major milestones you might have to pass in five years. Set some goals for this year. And then move back to the present. What must you do today to begin your journey?

Testing Your Story

In front of you is a plan for the future, a new story. Is that the exact way it will happen? Very unlikely! You know that plans aren't set in concrete. Good plans show us one way to go. You start out that way, check your progress, and make necessary changes and modifications as you go. You keep the goal in view. Sometimes you make it. Sometimes it turns out better or worse than you hoped and planned. Why then do you make goals and plans? Goals tell you what you want to be. They carve out a picture of the future that not only tells you what you want to do, but also tells you what you don't want to do. That may not be the way things turn out, but that's not the point. Let me give an example.

When I was fifty I went through this process. I decided when I was 65 I wanted to be teaching in a graduate school and doing management consulting. For many good reasons that's not completely where I was fifteen years later. But laying out those plans and checking progress along the way showed me the kind of life I would like to lead, the kind of person I would like to be. It also helped me to share my hopes and dreams with others so they could walk the journey with me. And it forced me to assess my values and decide what was important in life, what might best reflect the story of Jesus' life.

The last test for the worth and possibility of this new story takes you back to your beginning. Will this story end with that satisfaction that comes with "Well done, good and faithful servant!" (Matt. 25:21)? Will you be satisfied that you are a success?

If you plan to be in business, is the business one where you can live out your kingdom values? Is the rest of your life a whole? Is business part of life or all of it? Does this story reflect a growing faith, an expanding experience of God's grace and love? Do you have the faith to believe not only that this is God's best for you, but also that God wants to see it happen and therefore it will?

If your answers are not all "yes," go back and do your planning again. One of the great things about fantasizing in prayer is that no harm has been done. Nothing happens until you take a first step.

Writing a Story with Others

When you believe your plan is right, test it with other people. That's not easy. It may almost seem like bragging, or perhaps you feel that your ambitions will be seen as too small. We all need people with whom we feel safe, people who have demonstrated the love of God flowing through them to us. That's why your new life story must include other people.

All of life is lived in relationships. We are either for them or against them. Mr. Scrooge of Dickens' *Christmas Carol* was against relationships. His view was that all people were his adversaries. All of us have a little of Scrooge in us. This tendency to avoid relationships violates what Jesus described as the primary commandment: Love one another. Archbishop of Canterbury William Temple saw "original sin" demonstrated in every newborn who sees himself or herself as the center of the universe. All of life revolves around this one person. A baby experiences only his or her needs and has no concern or thought for others. Maturing in Christ, growing in faith, is a process where we see ever more clearly that God is the center of the universe, and we find ourselves in him, and we experience him in others.

Your pilgrimage as a Christian is a journey in relationships. God fitted you to be in relationship with other people. You are gifted as an individual, but you have also been gifted for life in the Body. Your relationships move out like a series of circles. The core is your relationship with Jesus Christ. The next circle is your relationship with your family, then to your friends, to your local church, and to the world beyond that.

Perhaps the most difficult part of your new beginning is to share the vision with someone else. What if you fail? What if you change your mind? What will other people think? And it may very well be that the Christians around you are just as much sucked into this business of worldly success as you are. But God operates through his Spirit in the hearts and minds of Christians everywhere. The beginning of a new journey for you may be the catalyst which helps other people to begin their new journey.

So if you are married, share with your spouse the excitement of this new story you have written. Explain what you have learned and what God seems to be saying to you. Encourage feedback. If your spouse has never struggled with these things, ask how he or she would plan for a better future, one in which God is glorified and you are enjoying him together.

You dare not take this journey alone. Frank Sinatra made famous a song titled "My Way." It was the quintessence of individualism. I don't need anybody but myself. I don't need you. The cards were stacked against me, but I did it my way, and I won! Christian success stories don't turn out that way! Plan to enlist other men and women to take the journey with you. This is not as hard as you might think. Americans are skilled at using self-help groups, and the church has a great deal to learn from what is going on in secular society. Perhaps you know four or five other individuals or couples who have expressed a desire to have a better image of the future. If you enter into a covenant group with these people, a group that promises to support one another and to shape one another and to help one another along on the journey, you will discover a whole new dimension of Christian life. Read this book together. Discuss your answers to the questions. What an exciting thing to watch others step out in faith with you!

Putting It on the Calendar

What we call a calendar—that little date book or folder you carry around—the British call a diary. Americans think of a diary as a record of things that have already happened. Our date book is a record of things we hope will happen or expect to happen. It too is a statement of faith. We don't know if we will even be alive when the date arrives. But look at your date book. What new things will have to happen if this story is to be fulfilled? More time with your family? A different work schedule? More research? I like date books that have a Things-to-Do list for every day. What goals need to be accomplished by a certain day? Write in specific times and places. Go out as far as you can.

Look before Leaping

Ideas are but pale ghosts until they are acted on. Your new story may begin with something as simple as redefining how you make decisions at work to something as drastic as deciding you need to quit your job and do something entirely different.[2] If it is a dramatic first step, you must be prepared for the immediate consequences.

Why not just do what you know God wants you to do and trust him for the future? Good question. There are a number of answers. The first is found in the process you went through. In trying to think God's thoughts after him for your future, you had a lifetime in view. While you fantasized in prayer, you had to imagine the various scenarios that might follow after you did something drastic, like quitting your job. (Again, remember that all statements about the future are statements of faith. You may have it wrong, or God may have something even better for you.) Second, God wants us to be responsible—responsible to use all the information and intelligence we have and to be responsible for the people who share our lives.

I have counseled people not to delay quitting a job that was discovered to be part of an immoral business. They took my advice and the immediate financial consequences were serious. But if we are living in sin or contributing to the sin of others, we should run from the sinful situation regardless of the future. But that is not a common situation. Here we have been thinking through a new story to its end.

Finally, there is nothing especially spiritual or pleasing to God in staying blind to the future. It often takes much more courage to act when we *know* the possible consequences than when we do not.

Step Out with Confidence

The journey of a thousand miles starts with one step. Confidently take the first steps. Report back to your support group. Pray with your spouse if you are married. Use your prayer journal to tell God what happened. What are you learning? Are new values conflicting with the old ones? What are you going to do about that? Can you stay on this course for six months, a year? If you can, press on. If you can't, go back and reflect on what you have learned. Revise your plan. You are trying something you have never done before. Don't be surprised that you are not an expert in one week. Think of it as a new job. No job ever turns out like the person who took it thought it would. It's always different. A lot of learning must take place, whether you come on board as a junior worker or the CEO. Sure you may have a track record, but that's in a different place. This is a new story.

Figure 3

Planning My New Life

Project	Date I Will Do This
Spend 4 to 8 hours fantasizing in prayer, setting goals for 15, 10, and 5 years.	
Spend 4 hours deciding what I want to be doing one year from now.	
Spend 4 hours planning actions for the coming month.	
Review plan to analyze what values it expresses.	
Revise plan as necessary.	
Share my dreams with my spouse and family.	
Share my dreams and goals with supporting Christians.	
Revise plan as necessary.	
Act.	
Reevaluate.	

Reflection

I hope you have already put a date on your calendar to do the first exercise in writing a new story by fantasizing in prayer. Figure 3 will help you list starting dates. Your experience as a business person tells you that plans need to be reviewed regularly. So do your plans. Remember, a better plan may come along! Look for it. Expect it.

Figure 3 on page 201 shows a list of dates to get you started. When will you do them?

It is one thing to write a different story about the rest of your life. It is quite another to live it. These guidelines will help:

Keep your promises. If other people find you dependable, they will help along the way.

Rely on the body of Christ. The Christian life is a life lived in relationships. You can't go it alone.

Find a mentor. There are men and women who will be honored to share their experience with you.

Keep a journal. Tell God and yourself how the story is turning out and what needs to be changed.

Study the Word. That's the ultimate authority.

Pray. It's the only way to keep all the pieces in their proper places.

12

Living a Different Story

So much for how to *discover* a different story. Are there common characteristics to every Christian story? Certainly each of us lives a unique life. In all of God's creation, there is no one like you. But there are some biblical givens that need to be included in every person's story. The suggestions that follow incorporate that truth. They provide a way of integrating your roles, your values, your future.

Keep Your Promises

Lewis Smedes has helped me a great deal in understanding the unbelievable significance of making a promise. A promise is a commitment for the future. Not much point in making promises about yesterday! A promise is very much like a goal. Both lie in the future. Both are statements about what I expect to happen. But a promise goes further than a goal. A promise says, "Within my ability and if circumstances don't stop me, I will do what I have said I will do." In recent years I have modified the business principle of management-by-objectives so it is more like management-by-promise-keeping.

There is something so much more ethically profound about making a promise as compared to committing to an objective. In business we are accustomed to being asked to do things and asking others to do things. If it's our boss who is doing the asking, we may agree even though we are not sure it's a very good idea. We may take on the task half-heartedly and perhaps find excuses why it shouldn't be done. On the other side of the coin, we make excuses for people who don't do what they said they would. Shifting our thinking to seeing a commitment to the future as a promise given and received can change our entire attitude about life. Let me recommend it to you as a business practice. There is no higher commendation that can be given to a business person than to say that he or she keeps promises. That applies in big and little things. In our culture it implies arriving on time, completing an assignment when it is due, producing quality work.

There is an ultimate promise we need to talk about. Of all the commitments we make, it is the only one that we make for life. It is the promise we give when as a couple we come before a pastor and exchange our marriage vows. It is the only promise we make that includes "until death do us part." I realize that in a day when many marriages seem like trial arrangements, such an idea sounds old-fashioned, out of step with the times. But it is the times that are out of step. God's design was that marriage should signify the commitment that Christ has made to his church (Eph. 5:22–33). The promise is "I will give you 100 percent. My dedication will not be conditioned on what you give in return. This is no 50-50 arrangement. I promise all of myself to you."

Family

There is another promise we make that doesn't have the lifetime duration and impact that marriage does, but it is closely related. When you have children, you make a promise to them. You promise to house and feed them, to educate and train them. You promise to be a model for them, to love them and to give them time. In a day of two-income families this is not easy. Society is coming to realize that the primary danger to the family is the absent father, regardless of the reasons for his absence. Children need a father, a male role model.

What might that entail? For one thing, time. Schedule family devotional times. Get a Bible story book and read to your children every morning at breakfast (even if you or they have to get up early!). When that one is worn out, buy another one. Teach them Bible verses that speak of hope, joy, and caring.

Rely on the Body of Christ

I suspect that the New Testament writers never contemplated a "church" with three thousand members. Without arguing the point for small churches or house churches or even Peter Wagner's description of the celebration, the congregation, and the cell as being three levels within a large church, let me urge you to find, develop, create, get into a small support group. You need other Christians. You can't live a successful life alone. None of us have all the gifts and resources we need. That's why Christ describes us as his body with each part interdependent. The foot cannot say to the hand, "Because I am not a hand, I am not part of the body" (1 Cor. 12:15). We all need each other. To talk about a "successful Christian" who is not integrally related to other believers is a contradiction in terms.

In Louis Evans's guide to groups, *Covenant to Care*, he describes various ways people might covenant together to lend mutual support. I have found that developing such a covenant before starting a group is important. It gives a natural opportunity to discuss the meaning of this covenant. There is a normal tendency in groups to go no deeper than the willingness of the most reticent member. You need to go deeper! You need to be able to discuss the ethical dilemmas of life and tell each other your hurts, your failures. You need people who will hold you accountable to do what you say you will do. That is where a covenant can help.

With whom do you begin? Perhaps with another Christian business person. See if there are two or three others with whom you can meet regularly. It is often easier to form a group of the same gender, but if you have that kind of a group, form one for couples also.

Find a Mentor

A mentor is someone to whom you look for regular guidance, a spiritual director. It should be someone of the same sex, someone older. What do you do with a mentor? What is it that you want? Perhaps your primary need is to have someone see you through the business decisions that you make. Perhaps you need a spiritual director, someone with whom you can share your doubts and ask your frank questions. The first time you get together you could discuss a problem or situation that is vexing you. After two or three meetings you will find all kinds of things to talk about.

How do you find a mentor? It is surprisingly easy. Observe the people around you. Look for the person you admire the most. Go to that person and say, "I need an older person to talk to about my life. You really impress me as someone from whom I can learn a lot. Would you be willing to meet with me on a regular basis and mentor me?"

You will probably be pleasantly surprised at the response. People are complimented, even flattered, by being asked to give counsel. Even if a person has to decline, you have made a friend. Ted Engstrom's *The Fine Art of Mentoring* is an excellent source of information.

Journaling

Journals can take many forms. Years ago I purchased an 8-1/2 x 11 loose leaf New Testament. It had just one column of print down the side of the page, leaving two-thirds of the page for notes. I determined that I was going to write down all the things that came to my mind about the passage—encouragements, doubts, disbelief, blessings—all of it. It was an intimidating experience. There are a number of different ways of going about building a journal.

Journaling is different from keeping a diary. Yes, there may be some daily occurrences recorded, but the purpose is to write down your reflections about what is going on in your life: your joys, your doubts, your needs. That is why journaling and praying and reading God's Word are so closely related. You are trying to be as honest as you possibly can with yourself and with the Lord. What is he saying to you? What is your response? What should you be doing about it?

Does the journaling process uncover values you are having trouble maintaining? What are they? What can you do about them? Save them for discussion with your mentor. Consider talking about them in your small group. Encourage others to do the same.

Ask the Lord for specific things. Note the date when you asked and look forward to answers. Use the same journal to describe your dreams about the future. Think of it as your Life Book. When you fill one book, get another.

Study the Word

"When in doubt, read the directions."

"Of course," you say, "all Christians should be studying the Bible." But few are. Here we are, claiming that we want to be successful Christians, and many of us are not reading the directions. We collect a bunch of rules as to how Christians are supposed to act, but they are secondhand rules. They have been filtered through others' experiences. Nothing wrong with that, but the day will come when we need our own unique understanding, and a primary way God gives us that is through knowledge of his Word.

Bible study is different from listening to God through his Word. That often happens when we are studying the Bible, but that's not the main purpose. I suspect that if there is one thing that Satan really wants to discourage, it is Bible study. No one has completely mastered God's Word. The Bible is a collection of writings that spans hundreds of years. Through the ages students and scholars have gained powerful insights into its meaning and its interrelationships. Read all the commentary material you can, but don't neglect the basic text. One of the best ways of getting a broad grasp is to try to master one book. In chapter 8 we let the Book of Matthew give us an overview of life in the kingdom of God. While I have probably taught that book more than any other, I always learn something new. An effective way to learn anything is to *teach* it. Accepting the task of a Sunday school teacher or Bible study leader will give you a higher incentive to learn more.

Pray

There are many different approaches to prayer. Some people manage to have an on-going dialogue with God all day. Others find it necessary to consciously bring themselves into God's presence. Decide on a special time and place where each day you will encounter God through his Word and in conversation. Don't make excuses for yourself! You manage to get to work on time, don't you? You usually appear for dinner. You put dates in your date book. Make some dates with God. How can we expect to find success in God's kingdom if we never talk to the King?

Use Your Calendar

We live in a society driven by appointments. You can retire to a mountain cabin and get away from it all, but if you are going to continue in the world of business, you must fit into society's timetable. Stores do open and close. Trains and planes more or less leave on time. Business hours are fixed. TV programs begin on the hour or half-hour. Schools start the same time every day.

Imagine a month with no appointments. Start logging on your calendar the most important things first. What might they be? It's rather obvious that your most important appointment is with God. "Oh," you might say, "I don't have to put *that* down." Fine! If that is a habit with you, don't write it in. You are a magnificent minority! Most of us need to mark it down. How much time? How much time do you need? Start with fifteen minutes each morning. Do that for a week. Move up to twenty. See what God does in your life to make more time for him.

Dates with your family come next. Dates with your spouse, even if it is only a quiet half-hour talking together at the end of the day. Dates with your kids. Aren't they just as important as everyone else? Dates with your mentor. Dates for your support group. At this point you are thinking that with all these dates you will have no time to go to *work*! Yes, you will. That new story you have written about a successful life depends on these human relationships. Get those right, and the rest will fall into place.

Consider a family calendar. Find a place where you can put a monthly calendar where everyone in the family will put down his or her plans. Discuss with the family when you will have family times. When will you take a vacation? When will you and your spouse be away enjoying one another? When will you have to be out of town or at a meeting?

Bon Voyage!

We have come to the end of our journey together. The rest is up to you. You can respond: "It's just too tough. I don't have what it takes to live an integrated Christian life," or, "Yes, I can see how that's possible, but I don't have the faith to make it happen."

No, you haven't. But God is with you. There are thousands of men and women who have discovered that God is able, and not only able, but also lovingly wanting to change their lives. I like Phillips translation of a familiar verse in Ephesians 4: "Live life then, with a due sense of responsibility, not as men [and women!] who do not know the meaning and purpose of life but as those who do" (Eph. 4:15).

Endnotes

Chapter 2

1. Peter Drucker differentiates between business, government, and nonprofit organizations: "Business supplies either goods or services. Government controls. A business has discharged its task when the customer buys the product, and is satisfied with it. Government has discharged its function when its policies are effective. The 'nonprofit' institution neither supplies goods or services nor controls. Its product is neither a pair of shoes nor effective regulation. Its product is a *changed human being.*" (See Peter F. Drucker, *Managing the Nonprofit Organization*, p. xiv.)

2. In researching this book it became obvious that Christians who are CEOs face a wholly different set of questions than those who have a lesser responsibility for the company's affairs. Theoretically, CEOs have the power to make the needed changes that their Christian conscience may dictate.

3. In 1988 in the 700-plus United States Protestant foreign mission agencies the median income was $250,000 per year, financially the size of a medium-size drugstore.

4. Louis Allan in his *Professional Management* helps us to understand that there is a difference between "technical work" and "management work."

Chapter 4

1. *As You Like It,* Act II, Scene 7, Line 139.
2. *Macbeth,* Act V, Scene 5, Line 11.

Chapter 5

1. An underground best-seller for many years on this subject was Edward Stewart's *American Cultural Patterns: A Cross-Cultural Perspective.* The revised edition, done with Milton Bennett, is even better.

2. For a fuller discussion see Edward R. Dayton, *What Ever Happened to Commitment?*

3. *Democracy in America.*

4. Quoted from Cotton Mather's "Two Brief Discourses," Robert L. Heilbroner and Aaron Singer, *The Economic Transformation of America,* p. 13.

5. See Peter Drucker, *Managing the Nonprofit Organization.*

6. This is the common complaint of Latin Americans who believe that the citizens of the United States have no idea of the negative effects of American capitalism on their countries. They see us as people whose per capita consumption of the world's natural resources strips them of their share. In spite of all the U.S. aid that has gone to Latin America, the net flow of capital has always been from Latin America to North America.

7. De Tocqueville, *Democracy in America,* 2:72.

8. George Barna, *The Frog in the Kettle,* pp. 113, 114.

9. What follows is drawn from Edward R. Dayton, *What Ever Happened to Commitment,* p. 107f.

10. Jonathan Edwards, *The Works of President Edwards* (10 volumes, New York, 1829), vol. IV, p. 128, as quoted in H. Richard Niebuhr, *The Kingdom of God in America,* p. 141.

11. Russell Rickey and Donald Jones, *American Civil Religion,* p. 57.

12. The use of the term is attributed to Robert Bellah. See his *The Broken Covenant: American Civil Religion in Time of Trial.*

Chapter 6

1. For further reading see H. Shelton Smith, Robert T. Handy, and Lefferts A. Loetscher, *American Christianity* or another comprehensive study of church history.

2. Smith, et al., *American Christianity,* vol. 1, p. 314.

3. Ibid., p. 315.

4. See Sidney Mead, *The Lively Experiment.*

5. See George Marsden, *The History of Fundamentalism in America.*

6. Ibid.

7. George Hunter's book *Communicating the Christian Faith to Secular People* gives good insight in to how to breach this secular wall.

Chapter 7

1. See Philip Schaff, *The Creeds of Christendom.*

2. Oliver F. Williams and John W. Houck, *Full Value: Cases in Christian Business Ethics.*

Chapter 8

1. This is not to deny the power of television to preach the gospel and bring people to Christ. Nor is it meant to denigrate the value of a "television church" for the bedridden. In the former case, one hopes that a person will be drawn to a local body of believers. In the second case, one would hope that the person was also ministered to by flesh-and-blood Christians in his or her community.

Chapter 9

1. Richard J. Foster, *Freedom of Simplicity,* p. 17f.

Chapter 10

1. For more on covenant groups, see Louis Evans Jr.'s *Covenant to Care.*

Chapter 11

1. For an excellent discussion on the healing power of goals, see Ari Kiev, *Strategy for Daily Living.*

2. Ibid.

3. *What Color Is Your Parachute?* is revised periodically. It is an excellent guide to thinking through to a new job.

Bibliography

Abraham, William J. *The Logic of Evangelism*. Grand Rapids: Wm. B. Eerdmans, 1989.

Allen, Louis. *Professional Management*. New York: McGraw-Hill, 1973.

Bellah, Robert. *The Broken Covenant*. New York: Seabury, 1976.

Barna, George. *The Frog in the Kettle*. Ventura, Calif.: Regal Books, 1990.

————. *User Friendly Churches*. Ventura, Calif.: Regal Books, 1991.

————. *What Americans Believe*. Ventura, Calif.: Regal Books, 1991.

Blamires, Harry. *The Christian Mind*. Ann Arbor: Servant Books, 1978 (American Edition).

Bolles, Richard. *What Color Is Your Parachute?* Berkeley, Calif.: Ten Speed Press, 1990.

Bonhoeffer, Dietrich. *Ethics*. New York: Macmillan, 1955.

Bly, Robert. *Iron John*. New York: Addison-Wesley Publishing Company, 1990.

Bradshaw, John. *Bradshaw on the Family*. Deerfield Beach, Fla.: Health Communications, 1988.

Carnell, Edward J. *The Case for Orthodox Theology*. Philadelphia: Westminster Press, 1959.

————. *Christian Commitment*. New York: Macmillan, 1957.

Dalby, Gordon. *Healing the Masculine Soul*. Waco: Word, 1990.

Dayton, Edward R. *God's Purpose/Man's Plans*. Monrovia, Calif.: MARC, 1973.

————. *What Ever Happened to Commitment?* Grand Rapids: Zondervan, 1984.

————. *That Everyone May Hear*. Monrovia, Calif.: MARC, 1981.

Dayton, Edward R., and Ted W. Engstrom. *Strategy for Living*. Ventura, Calif.: Regal Books, 1976.

de Tocqueville, Alexis. *Democracy in America,* Phillips Bradley, ed., (2 vols.). New York: Alfred A. Knopf, 1945.

Diebold, John. *The Role of Business in Society*. New York: AMA, 1982.

Drucker, Peter F. *The Practice of Management*. New York: Macmillan, 1954.

————. *Managing the Nonprofit Organization*. New York: HarperCollins, 1990.

Evans, Louis, Jr. *Covenant to Care*. Wheaton: Victor Books, 1982.

Foster, Richard J. *Freedom of Simplicity*. San Francisco: Harper & Row, 1981.

Hardy, Lee. *The Fabric of This World*. Grand Rapids: Wm. B. Eerdmans, 1990.

Harris, Thomas A. *I'm O.K. You're O.K.* New York: Harper & Row, 1967.

Heilbroner, Robert L., and Aaron Singer. *The Economic Transformation of America*. New York: Harcourt, Brace, Jovanovich, 1972.

Henry, Carl F. H. *The Uneasy Conscience of Modern Fundamentalism*. Grand Rapids: Wm. B. Eerdmans, 1947.

————. *Remaking of the Modern Mind*. Grand Rapids: Wm. B. Eerdmans, 1946.

Hunter, George. *Communicating the Christian Faith to Secular People.* Nashville: Abingdon, 1991.

Hunter, James Davidson. *Evangelicalism: The Coming Generation.* University of Chicago Press, 1987.

Hybels, Bill. *Too Busy Not to Pray.* Downers Grove, Ill.: InterVarsity Press, 1988.

Kier, Ari. *Strategy for Daily Living.* New York: Free Press, 1973.

Kraybill, Donald. *The Upside-Down Kingdom.* Scottdale, Pa.: Herald Press, 1978.

Ladd, George E. *Jesus and the Kingdom.* New York: Harper & Row, 1964.

Levinson, Daniel J. *The Seasons of a Man's Life.* New York: Alfred A. Knopf, 1978.

MacNutt, Francis A. *Healing.* Alamonte Springs: Strang Communications Co., 1988.

Marquand, John. *Point of No Return.* Chicago: Academy Chicago Publications, 1985.

Marsden, George. *Fundamentalism and American Culture.* New York: Oxford University Press, 1980.

———. *Reforming Fundamentalism.* Grand Rapids: Wm. B. Eerdmans, 1987.

Maslow, Abraham. *Motivation and Personality.* Rev. New York: Harper & Row, 1970.

Mead, Sidney. *The Lively Experiment.* New York: Harper & Row; 1976.

Morgan, Gareth. *Images of Organization.* Newberry Park, Calif. 1986.

Neustadt, Richard E., and Ernest R. May. *Thinking in Time.* New York: The Free Press, 1988.

Newbigin, Lesslie. *The Gospel in a Pluralist Society.* Grand Rapids: Wm. B. Eerdmans, 1989.

Peck, Scott. *The Road Less Traveled.* New York: Simon & Schuster, 1978.

Richey, Russel E., and Donald G. Jones, eds. *American Civil Religion*. New York: Harper & Row, 1974.

Schaff, Philip. *The Creeds of Christendom* (3 vols.). Grand Rapids: Baker Book House, 1966.

Schumacher, Christian. *To Live and Work: A Theological Interpretation*. MARC, 1987.

Sheey, Gail. *Passages*. New York: E. P. Dutton and Co., 1971.

Sine, Tom. *Why Settle for More and Miss the Best?* Waco: Word, 1987.

Skinner, B. F. *Beyond Freedom and Dignity*. New York: Alfred A. Knopf, 1971.

Skillen, James W. *The Scattered Voice*. Grand Rapids: Zondervan, 1990.

Smedes, Lewis. *Mere Morality*. Grand Rapids: Wm. B. Eerdmans, 1983.

Smith, H. Shelton, Robert T. Handy, and Lefferts A. Loetscher. *American Christianity*. New York: Charles Scribner & Sons, 1960.

Stapleton, Ruth Carter. *The Gift of Inner Healing*. Waco: Word, 1976.

Stewart, Edward C., and J. Bennett Milton. *American Cultural Patterns: A Cross-Cultural Perspective*. Rev. Yarmouth, Maine: Intercultural Press, 1991.

Stott, John. *Involvement*. Old Tappan, N.J.: Fleming R. Revell, 1985.

Turkel, Studs. *Working*. New York: Ballantine, 1985.

Webber, Robert E. *The Secular Saint*. Grand Rapids: Zondervan, 1979.

Weiss, Richard. *The American Myth of Success*. New York: Basic Books, 1969.

Williams, Oliver F., and John W. Houck. *Full Value: Cases in Christian Business Ethics*. New York: Harper & Row, 1978.

Wills, Gary. *Under God*. New York: Simon and Schuster, 1990.

Waterman, Robert H., Jr., and Thomas J. Peters. *In Search of Excellence*. New York: Harper & Row, 1982.

Appendix

Reflections: A Workbook

Chapter 1 What Is Success?

1. Write the following descriptions on four different pieces of paper: First, what do you think other people think of you? Who do they say you are? Second, who do *you* think you are? Third, what and who would you like to be? Fourth, who do you think God would like you to be?

2. Read over your responses to these four questions. What do they tell you about your current perception of what it means to be successful?

3. If possible, do this assignment with a trusted friend (or better yet a group of friends). Share your answers. You will be pleasantly surprised how much you discover about each other.

Chapter 2 What Is Business?

1. How large is the business for which you are working?

2. How long have you worked there?

3. How much influence do you have on the decisions that it makes?

4. Is your business considered a leader in its field?

5. What impact is the industry of which your business is a part having on the way it makes decisions?

6. Would you consider that your business is most interested in profit as a bottom line, or is it interested in some other results?

7. What do the answers to these questions tell you about your chances of "success" as it is measured by the business of which you are a part?

8. Why do you think *you* work? What is the most important reason? Is it fun?

9. If you are working through this book in a group setting, (or if you have a friend whose judgment you trust), ask if they think this is the best job for you. If so, why? If not, why not?

Chapter 3 What Is Faith?

1. What are the absolute truths in your life?

2. Think about your last few weeks at work. What happened in your life there that you feel doesn't jibe with Christian ethics?

3. What things happened in your company that didn't square with the Ten Commandments or the Sermon on the Mount?

4. What is going on in your industry that might not be happening if Jesus was setting the rules?

5. To what extent is your business life different from your "Christian" life? Why do you think this is so?

6. What does your performance at work tell you about your faith? Are you applying the same values on the job as elsewhere in your life?

7. As others share their answers with you, what do *their* answers tell you about your own situation?

Chapter 4 Today's Workplace

1. List the roles that are a daily part of your life. Are there rules in one role that have nothing to do with another? (If you are working with a group, combine your lists to make a composite picture.)

2 Is there a common set of rules that you apply to all of your roles? If not, why not?

3. How are the rules or values different at your business from what they are at home or church?

4. In what way do your various roles keep you from leading a *Christian* life?

5. What would have to happen for you to have the "mind of Christ" in all your roles?

6. Go back and look at the four descriptions you wrote at the end of chapter 1. Note particularly the one that described how you would like others to know you. What roles do you play in this one?

Chapter 5 Today's Society and Its Values

Seven American values are listed below. After each one write a one-sentence statement on how this value affects your personal view of success, business, or faith.

1. Pluralism

2. Equality

3. Individualism

4. Materialism

5. Competitiveness

6. Capitalism

7. Civil religion

Chapter 6 Today's Church

1. Are you a member of a local church? If not, why not? If not, how do you get support from fellow Christians?

2. What are the positive features of your local church, those things that help you sort through the meaning of life in general and life in the workplace?

3. Look at the list of needs on page 122. Are any of them your needs? What other needs do you have that are not being met by the church?

4. Based on your reading and your "assignments" thus far, do you think you can find success on your own? If not, how could the church be helping?

Chapter 7 Today's Christian

1. Are there other Christians in your company? How many of them do you know personally?

2. To what extent have you discussed with other Christians the dilemmas of matching your faith with your performance on the job, as well as the company's performance?

3. What do you think would happen if you brought together a group of Christians within your company to discuss "Christian values"? What resources would you need? How would you go about discussing what Christian values are?

Chapter 8 Life in God's Kingdon

1. Look through this chapter and make a list of kingdom values.

2. How do the values of the kingdom of God differ from what you have heard about the Christian life?

3. In what ways do these kingdom values diverge from your business values?

4. To the extent that they are different, what aspects of kingdom life will help you let the values of the kingdom predominate at work?

5. If you tried to work out kingdom values in your life, how would that change your definition of success?

Chapter 9 Values to Live By

1. What does it mean to you to "Go hard after God"?

2. What are the idols in your life that you may be putting in the place of God?

3. Are there other ways of misusing the name of the Lord besides swearing? Which ones might you be guilty of?

4. Is getting your job done sometimes more important than your relationships? What are some examples of that?

5. Is there a balance between your relationships at home and your relationships at work? Do your family members think so?

6. Are there ways in which your business can harm other people?

7. Are you tempted to have extramarital relationships on the job? What can you do to reduce that temptation?

8. Does your company ever steal anything from others? Do *you* steal anything from your company?

9. Does office gossip or company policy damage people's integrity?

10. What dissatisfactions in your life are related to seeing what other people have? Are they really important? What do you do to satisfy those wants? Is it worth the effort?

11. Does your church have a statement of faith, bylaws, or other descriptions of what its members stand for? Are you able to practice them on the job? If not, why not?

12. In what way has love become or not become your dominant value?

Chapter 10 Moving into the Future

1. Do you really believe God is for you? In what ways have you learned to trust God? What more do you yet have to learn?

2. In what way do the different parts of your life conflict with one another?

3. What roles are you playing? What are the values associated with them? Use the chart on page 187.

4. In what way do the world's values clash with the values you desire?